NEW EDITION

EMERGENCY

PREPAREDNESS

A PRACTICAL GUIDE FOR PREPARING YOUR FAMILY

EVAN GABRIELSEN

HORIZON PUBLISHERS

AN IMPRINT OF CEDAR FORT, INC.
SPRINGVILLE, UTAH

ISBN: 978-0-88290-985-1

Published by Horizon Publishers, an imprint of Cedar Fort, Inc.
2373 W. 700 S., Springville, UT, 84663
Distributed by Cedar Fort, Inc., www.cedarfort.com

Library of Congress Cataloging-in-Publication Data

Gabrielsen, Evan M.
 Emergency preparedness : a practical guide for preparing your family / Evan M. Gabrielsen.
  -- Second edition.
    pages cm
 Includes index.
 ISBN 978-0-88290-985-1
 1. Survival--Handbooks, manuals, etc. 2. Emergencies--Handbooks, manuals, etc. 3. Families--Handbooks, manuals, etc. 4. Emergency management--Handbooks, manuals, etc. I. Title.
 GF86.G33 2013
 613.6'9--dc23
                              2013010209

Cover design by Erica Dixon
Cover design © 2013 by Lyle Mortimer
Edited and typeset by Casey J. Winters

Printed in the United States of America

10 9 8 7 6 5 4 3 2 1

To my late father,
who taught me most of these principles.

And to my wife,
whose feedback and advice improved
this book immeasurably.

CONTENTS

PART 2:
Responding to Emergencies

PART 3:
Emergency Preparedness as a Way of Life

INTRODUCTION TO THE SECOND EDITION

Good for you! Just picking up this book and opening it shows that you are willing to take responsibility for your own survival. As you will see, attitude is half the battle. The other half is doing something about it, and here is where this book can help.

Since the first edition of this book was published in 1999, just prior to the Y2K scare, the world has changed. A grim morning in September 2001 changed our perspective of what threats we might face; evidence of a warming climate makes us brace for ever more powerful storms; and government help in Louisiana became almost as big a disaster as the disaster that precipitated it.

But technology has advanced in those years as well. Meteorologists are able to predict the paths of large storms days in advance, a huge improvement from January 1888, when the Schoolhouse Blizzard hit the Great Plains so unexpectedly that it caught and killed hundreds of people, many of whom were children between their schools and home. Satellite surveillance of weather systems is continuous. We now get most of our weather and news (and all information, really) from a handy little invention called the Internet, though the quality and accuracy must be watched closely, and our whole world revolves around phones so capable, we call them "smart." It is truly remarkable that during the East Coast Superstorm Sandy of October 2012, people were messaging each other about losing power; the social media site Twitter was more reliable than the power grid. And yet, when the power grid goes down, our phone batteries eventually run down, and our access to all of that helpful information is cut off.

Have preparedness principles also changed? What is important? Where do you start? With a practical common-sense guide, of course. I have sorted through much information from many sources and distilled key elements and described them in a practical way. For example, in my files I have no fewer than twenty differing lists of items that should go in a 72-hour kit. Some of the lists are frighteningly simplified (all you need is a pocketknife and your trusty loincloth), and some are impractically detailed (be sure to bring your implements for tanning hides). This is not an advanced, exhaustive book; this is a book of fundamentals to help you make a solid start. It is not a survival manual for when society collapses; it is a guide to making preparedness a way of life so you can ride out the little—and big—emergencies of life. This book summarizes, organizes, and focuses the important principles of each topic in a balanced, common-sense, everyday way.

The first part, "Emergency Preparedness Skills and Principles," includes basic topics and skills that are applicable to all emergencies. The second part, "Responding to Emergencies," discusses how to prepare for, survive, and respond to an array of specific common emergencies. The third and last part, "Emergency Preparedness as a Way of Life," is about making emergency preparedness a low-key but regular part of your life. After you have read the information here, you will be better equipped to decide which of the many advanced information sources will suit your needs.

Much of the material in this book was first printed in the *South Valley Journal*, a monthly Utah paper dedicated to local events and concerns in the southern Salt Lake Valley. The information has been updated, and a significant amount of new material has been added. Each chapter began as a freestanding article, so you can benefit from reading this book in any order. If you have a specific interest or worry, start there. Pick up a pencil and underline passages or make notes in the margins. This is a practical guide and workbook, not an heirloom. If you like it, share it with your friends and family.

I do not believe in a hysterical approach to emergency preparedness. Yes, I might sell more books if the title was *Buy This Book or Die in the Apocalypse!* But it is not my intent to scare anyone into preparedness. When panic is the driver, the result may be incomplete; and when the emotion passes, the letdown could damage the resolve to keep going. Instead, this book is built on the "slow and steady" philosophy of Aesop's tortoise. Emergency preparation is not about doom and gloom. It is ultimately hopeful: by preparing, we gain some control over events that seem uncontrollable; by preparing, we become "survivors," a mental attitude that experts say is more important than any gear we could collect; by preparing, we banish fear and panic. And we enable ourselves to help family, friends, and neighbors. I believe in the fundamental goodness of humanity and in neighbors helping neighbors through the worst of the rough patches. I also believe that emergency preparedness has to be continuous—a way of life—but that it does not have to be perfect.

The basic principles found in the 1999 edition of this little book are still fundamentally sound: make preparation a low-key but ever-present part of your life; work at it day by day; make a plan; prepare a 72-hour kit; learn some Boy Scout skills; and pay attention to forecasts, warnings, and predictions. With these principles, a family can ride out terrorist attacks, superstorms, tsunamis, nuclear meltdowns, and, yes, zombie attacks, without expecting someone else to do for them what they have the time, the sense, and the resources to do for themselves.

So this is still a practical guide, and it still urges commonsense planning using fundamental principles. It still affirms that any preparation is better than no preparation so you aren't immobilized by the impossibility of perfection. And it still counsels:

Do one thing today.

PART 1
EMERGENCY PREPAREDNESS SKILLS AND PRINCIPLES

DO ONE THING TODAY

The Most Potent Advice

Emergency preparedness. The phrase evokes images of calamity, of privation, of wheat in the basement and guns in the closet. It represents uncertainty; it causes fear. Many people avoid emergency preparedness because to acknowledge it makes disaster seem certain. Others avoid it because it is intimidating and overwhelming. There are so many things to be done, so much to be organized, so much to be learned. Where do you start?

The chapters in this book ends with the same phrase:

"Emergency preparedness: do one thing today."

This is the most potent advice in the entire book. It is more potent than telling you how much water to store or how to secure your water heater or why earthquakes do the damage they do. It is more potent than a 72-hour kit list or a first-aid kit description. Why is it such useful advice? Here are nine reasons:

1. "The journey of a thousand miles begins with one step."

—Lao Tse

"Do one thing today" restates a universal principle: by the yard it's hard; by the inch it's a cinch. Henry Ford said, "Nothing is particularly hard if you divide it into small jobs." This universal principle enables ordinary people to accomplish extraordinary projects by doing a little bit at a time. It works for things other than emergency preparedness. It works for self-improvement. It works for engineering and construction projects. It works for writing books about emergency preparedness. It just works.

2. "Don't let life discourage you; everyone who got where he is had to begin where he was."

—Richard L. Evans

"Do one thing today" gives you a starting point. Complex tasks, like emergency preparedness, do not always have a clear beginning and end. The prospect of the task can be overwhelming and discouraging. But the principle of "do one thing today" gives you permission to start anywhere you are comfortable, just as long as you start.

3. "We cannot do everything at once, but we can do something at once."

—Calvin Coolidge

"Do one thing today" breaks the paralysis of procrastination, gets you moving, gives you momentum. And once you are moving, forward progress is easier to sustain. Once you are moving, the things that intimidate you don't seem so insurmountable. It's easier to face the bear than to worry about facing the bear.

4. "Have no fear of perfection—you'll never reach it."

—Salvador Dali

"Do one thing today" gives you permission to be imperfect and incomplete. You only have to be a little better than you were. This realization releases you from a potentially disabling obsession of perfection. You don't need to compare yourself with anyone else or some imagined standard. You only need to do what you can immediately see to do. You can start with a single thing. And then, as you do the simple things, it will become clear to you what the next goals should be.

5. "Perseverance is more prevailing than violence; and many things which cannot be overcome when they are

together, yield themselves up when taken little by little."

—*Plutarch*

Most worthwhile undertakings in this life are long-term projects where perseverance is more important than speed. "Do one thing today" is the mantra of the person who is in it for the long term. It acknowledges that emergency preparedness is not a fad of the week but an attitude for life.

6. "He is educated who knows how to find out what he doesn't know."

—*Georg Simmel*

"Do one thing today" is better than knowledge. If taken to heart, it supplies the motivation that will lead to knowledge.

7. "Diligence is the mother of good luck."

—*Benjamin Franklin*

"Do one thing today" is more effective than "do it all once and forget it." Emergency preparedness requires regular attention. If you constantly review and improve your supplies, you'll know what you have, and what you need. This knowledge will allow you to be resourceful instead of panicky. If you constantly review and improve your preparedness, it is easier to stay current on rotation and replacement schedules. As you continue to review and improve, you'll naturally tailor your efforts to changing needs and risks.

8. "Willful waste brings woeful want."

—*Thomas Fuller*

"Do one thing today" is cheaper than one-shot preparedness. You'll tailor your purchases to your own needs better than a pre-packed kit would. You'll be able to shop sales. You'll be more aware of opportunities. You will be more organized and orderly. Panic-buying is never cheap.

9. "Do one thing today" really works.

Scheduled Disasters, Convenient Emergencies, and Other Myths

All right, let's get started: everyone get out your calendar or daily planner and turn to the page that shows the next earthquake. What? It's not on there? Okay then, how about the next tornado? Hmm. Does anyone's calendar show a date for their next house fire? No? Hazardous material incident? No? What's the problem here? Surely it makes sense to schedule disasters and emergencies so we can get ready for them. But we can't predict the future; we cannot schedule disasters. Even worse, disasters occur when they occur, not when it is convenient for us.

Some might say, "Well, we can read conditions and determine that disasters are going to come. We pay attention to the news; we'll get some warning of social problems and wars and things like that." Okay, but earthquakes, tornados, hazardous material spills, dam failures, floods, avalanches, power outages, and so on all occur without having the common courtesy to warn us first, on local news stations or otherwise. Even in those cases when we get some advance notice, like hurricanes, droughts, volcanic activity, and social disorder, by the time the situation becomes clear, it is often too late to do serious preparing. Others might say, "The Bible gives us signs of impending calamities. The faithful will have warning." But this is the same Bible that gives us the parable of the ten virgins and the message that when the bridegroom comes, those without oil in their lamps will be left behind. Some might even say, "Oh, the Government will take care of me, and the schools will take care of my children," or, "My church or neighbors will take care of me."

If you haven't realized it yet, realize it now: preparedness is about taking personal responsibility for yourself and your family. While many people can help in small ways, no one else will take care of your family if you don't. The lesson is clear: we have to prepare before the disasters strike. We have to remain prepared all of the time.

What does it mean to be prepared all of the time? It means having the right knowledge, gear, and attitude on hand. It means everyone in your household must know what to do, since some of them may have to face an emergency alone. It means:

1. You learn—knowledge is the most versatile commodity, infinitely updatable, never out of style. Learn what emergencies you can expect in your area. Learn what they can do. Learn how to protect

yourself from them. Learn fire safety, learn how to store water and food, and learn first aid. Learn basic skills like safely starting a fire, cooking over a fire, cooking one-pot meals, cleaning up with a minimum of water, and so on.

2. Having some concrete plans for what you'll do in an emergency reduces the chances for panic. It also gives you the survivor's attitude that experts say is so important in weathering a crisis.

3. You establish a core of preparedness supplies. The best first step here is a basic 72-hour kit, including some water. A kit that contains supplies enabling your family to be self-sufficient for up to three days will get you through anything that requires an evacuation and through the first days of most other emergencies as well. There are any number of pre-assembled kits that can be quite complete, but you should always familiarize yourself with the contents and adapt them to your own specific needs.

4. Once you have a solid core of supplies, you can add items that are useful for your specific hazards. You could add an alternate source of heat if you live in a colder climate. You could add special kits for your kids' backpacks, your office, or your car. You could begin a program of long-term food storage to carry you through emergencies like unemployment or long-term recovery from an area devastation.

5. Finally, always being prepared means that you regularly update your preparedness: replace stored clothes as you outgrow them, rotate and replenish food and water to make sure they're ready when you need them, replace stored fuels and batteries as they become outdated, and so on. Updating is something that should become a low-key, but constant, part of your life.

People who have alternate types of lighting and heating won't be paralyzed by a power outage. People who have emergency gear and food on hand don't have to risk the mob scene at the stores. People who have emergency heating may be able to avoid frozen and broken pipes in an extended cold snap. People who have 72-hour kits assembled can evacuate more quickly, assured that they have the most important things. People who have some water and water purification stored can keep their families healthy if the water supply becomes contaminated or unavailable.

The short and painful truth is this: we don't know when our lives will be shaken up by a disaster. Although this seems to be a disadvantage about the way the world works, there are actually a number of positives associated with the unknowability of trouble:

- If everyone knew exactly when the next disaster was going to hit, many would still postpone their preparation until it was too late. Then, in addition to the disaster, we would have runs on stores, riots, and chaos. At least we're spared that roller-coaster ride.

- Not knowing when an emergency will occur requires that we be ready all of the time. Those who are prepared can live in this world with less fear of it.

- Being prepared, especially with some sort of food storage, can be a less expensive way to live.

- The lifestyle of preparation provides the perspective that life is more than just *this instant*. A longer view of life can enable the weathering of all of life's ups and downs with equanimity.

- The lifestyle of preparation is full of life-lessons for children. Frugality, saving for a rainy day, anticipating consequences of decisions—these are valuable lessons of maturity.

- If you are prepared yourself, you can assist friends, family, and neighbors. If not, you'll be so busy keeping your own family going that you won't be able to help anyone else who might need it.

Does constantly being prepared mean that you have to become a raving fanatic or camouflage-wearing bunker-builder? No, it just means thinking ahead and visualizing living your life after a disaster. And it means doing a little bit all of the time rather than a lot all at once and then nothing.

Emergency preparedness:
Do one thing today.
(Then do another thing tomorrow.)

THE SINGLE MOST IMPORTANT THING YOU CAN DO

Create a Family Emergency Plan

Get organized for emergencies by creating a family plan. There is no "correct" outline or content for a family plan. It is simply a collection of information and plans you have made with your own family. When you make your family plan, remember:

- Identify the most likely emergency situations in your area and get ready for those first. In my area—near Salt Lake City—house fires, earthquakes, hazardous material spills, and storm-related power failures are the most likely scenarios. Your area may have different hazards: local authorities and news stations can help you identify likely emergencies.

- Keep your plan short; no one can remember a lot of details, and you might forget things in a disaster.

- Write the plan down and post it where it can be seen: inside a closet door or on the refrigerator. You may also want small cards with key information like phone numbers and such that you give to each member of the family for backpacks, purses, wallets, and so on.

- Involve everyone in the family, including small children. Helping in the planning will help them remember the plan and will help them deal better emotionally with a disaster.

Your plan might include some of the following elements:

A Reunion Plan

First, identify the daily routines of everyone in the family. Where do you spend your time? At work, at school, at friends' houses, at the store, at the church? Discuss how you will get from each location to home in an emergency. Select a primary reunion location, like your home; then select a secondary reunion location out of the immediate area, in case you are not able to get home. Secondary locations might include churches, schools, or public buildings that everyone knows.

How will you get to the reunion location? What routes will you use, if passable? It would be a good idea to drive each of the routes looking for anything that might be a hidden hazard or make roads impassable like bridges, large power lines, and so on. Who will pick children up from school? What will you do if driving is not possible? If driving is not possible and it's too far to walk or the conditions make getting home unsafe, are there any nearby relatives, friends, or public shelters you can go to?

Considering the emergency plans and policies that schools have in place is important. Most schools will not allow anyone who is not on an approved list to pick up your child, even in an emergency. Many schools have plans in place so they can hold children at the school if needed. Some schools may have release policies. All schools want parents to know what is in their emergency response plans, so a quick phone call to the school will provide all of the relevant information here. And don't forget to read through the emergency plan at your place of work.

If children can walk home, plan a detailed route so that parents will know where to look for them. Avoid main traffic arteries or routes that have many electrical or water hazards. Practice walking the route with the children so they are familiar with it. You should also consider where the children will go if the parents are not home when they arrive. Coordinate with neighbors or relatives.

Each person in the family should also have a "get home bag" that includes good shoes and socks, a small water bottle, a high-energy snack, medications you may depend on, a photo of the family (for identification and comfort), and the ever-versatile bandanna (see chapter 32).

A Communication Plan

Even though you have a plan for getting back together, you will still want to contact your family to let them know you are all right. And no matter how thorough your planning, an emergency may require you to change your plans. Many disasters will make it difficult for you to contact each other directly: in Superstorm Sandy, high winds knocked out power lines, and storm surge flooding knocked out power—including cell phone nodes—to a large part of the coastal area. Communications by phone were impossible in the local area for some time. If evacuating, you may not even have access to a phone for a while. In an emergency, it may be easier to make long-distance calls than local ones. Identify a friend or relative outside of the immediate area or city (preferably outside the state) whom you can each call to relay messages. This contact person can act as a message board. Talk to your out-of-state contact in advance about what kind of information they should calmly extract—and write down—from each family member when they call: where they are, what time they called, where they are going, what route they will use, when they will call again, and so on. If cell phone calls are not going through, try sending a text, which uses less bandwidth, and it might make it through. Identifying two or three different contact people is a good idea, in case one of them is not home. In addition to the out-of-state contact, make a list of other neighbors and family you might call. Include parents' work numbers, nearby neighbors and family members, clergy, and day care. (It's a good idea to also include medical insurance plan information on this list.) Make sure everyone has a copy of the phone numbers (update frequently) and knows when and how to use them. This list should be written down and not simply programmed into a cell phone, which becomes useless when the battery runs out after a few hours. Although there are not many pay phones around, it might be smart to tape some phone money (quarters and dimes) to the list that has the phone numbers on it.

A "Get Ready" Plan

You already know a lot of things you could and should do to be more prepared for emergencies. Make a list and set some goals, with specific dates. You could have goals on:

- **Learning:** Check out emergency preparation sites on the Internet. Go to the library and see what resources they have. Take first-aid and CPR classes. Learn about local hazards and how to prepare from your police and fire departments and your utility companies.

- **Training:** Train everyone who is old enough to know how—and when—to turn off the utilities. Figure out your home fire escape plan; train and drill often. Have a "lights-out" practice.

- **Kits:** Put together a basic 72-hour kit. It doesn't have to be perfect—just get a start with what you have. Put together a car kit; your car is most likely to be somewhere near you in an emergency. Create mini-kits for pockets, purses, and backpacks. Organize all of your information on emergency preparedness into one place; put it in a binder. Assemble copies of your important papers and put them in a safe place. Make a written, video, or photo inventory of your household contents and put it in a safe place (safe-deposit box.) This will speed resolution of insurance claims.

• • •

The reason a family plan is the most important thing you can do is that it begins the discussion of what scenarios you want to prepare for and starts you thinking about how to get ready. You don't have to make a perfect family plan. Start with just one of the elements here and then add to it a little at a time. Your plan could even include elements that aren't listed here like long-term food storage or street safety training. The most important part of your plan is what your own family needs right now.

Sample Family Plan Outline

Primary Reunion Location Home	
If Mom and Dad Aren't Home Johnson's-: 123 Cedar, 555-0100	If Can't Get to the House Church-: 123 Main St. (by the south door)
Dad's Work ABC Co., 123 Park 555-0101 Cell-: 555-0102	Mom's Work State U, 123 Center 555-0103 Cell-: 555-0104
Dad's Route Home West on Park, South on I-100 Freeway, West on Main, South on Walnut	Mom's Route Home West on University, North on I-100 Freeway, West on Main, South on Pine, East on Spruce
Dad's Backup Location John Smith, 456 Park 555-0105	Mom's Backup Location Dr. Jones, 456 Center 555-0106

Bobby's School ABC Elementary, 123 Walnut, 555-0107 Pickup by Dad or Mrs. Johnson	Patty's School ABC Middle, 123 Spruce 555-0108 Pickup by Mom or Mrs. Brown
Bobby's Route Home South on Ash, East on Alder, South on Walnut	Patty's Route Home South on Pine, West on Maple, South on Walnut
Bobby's Backup Location Johnson's: 123 Cedar 555-0109	Patty's Backup Location Brown's 456 Spruce 555-0110

Out-of-State Contact: Grandma in California, 555-0111

Fire Escape Plan: Yes	Where to Meet? By Johnson's fence

Fire Practices and Smoke Alarm Tests: XJan. XApr. Jul. Oct.
Water Turnoff: XDad XMom XPatty XBobby
Gas Turnoff: XDad XMom Patty Bobby
Electricity Turnoff: XDad XMom Patty Bobby

72-Hour Kits: Front closet	72-Hour Kit Check up: XApr. Oct.

Goals for This Year: 1. Secure shelves 2. Teach Bobby and Patty how to turn off gas and electrical 3. Have a 24-hour practice (warm weather)
Other Phone Numbers: Aunt Mary (Aunt) 555-0112 Mr. Williams (Bishop) 555-0113 Mrs. Adams (Dad's Supervisor) 555-0114 Mrs. Petersen (Mom's Supervisor) 555-0115 Gonzalez (Neighbor) 555-0116 Hill (Neighbor) 555-0117

Emergency Plans for Seniors

We think of disasters as earthquakes, floods, blizzards—things that affect a wide area. But for elderly adults living independently, an additional set of personal crises can threaten their safety and independence: slips and falls, medication imbalance, crime, and even minor power outages that can affect medical equipment. If your family includes a senior member outside of your immediate neighborhood, you can do things right now to reduce vulnerability and keep in touch in an emergency. The following information is from the "IN TOUCH" plan developed by the Eldercare Locator, a national service funded by the Administration on Aging (www.eldercare.gov, 1-800-677-1116).

I—Identify Potential Emergency Situations

The first step is to identify the hazards or risks you are preparing for. Examine the residence. Look for fire risks, such as faulty wiring or overloaded circuits. Make sure smoke alarms work and are in good repair. Look for furniture that could topple in an earthquake. Check stairs, handrails, and especially bathrooms for slip and fall hazards. Repair loose handrails, and install non-slip rugs and grab bars if necessary. Don't forget to check outside as well. Look for crumbling concrete hazards or nearby trees or power lines that could damage the house. The insurance company can tell you if a residence is in a floodplain, and the age of the home indicates the level of earthquake it is designed to withstand. Learn about any predetermined evacuation routes and community emergency shelters.

N—Note Community Resources

The Eldercare Locator can put you in touch with services in the geographical area of your senior family member. These range from daily services, like Meals on Wheels, to services that assist with home repair and maintenance. Identify other informal community networks, such as churches, clubs, or senior centers frequented by your loved ones. Also identify neighbors or close friends who will be willing and able to assist in an emergency. Identify options for emergency pet care.

Write down a list of these contacts and contact information. They are your IN TOUCH team: medical professionals including doctors, pharmacists, and specialists; neighbors; friends; and contacts from agencies, churches, clubs, and senior centers. Include family contacts so the team can contact you. Also identify an out-of-state person whom both the senior and the family could check in with if a widespread emergency makes long distance calling easier than local.

T—Talk about Individual Circumstances

Remember that seniors have lifelong experience in dealing with emergencies. Work with each other to create this plan—don't just impose it. Also be sensitive about what outsiders you get involved with personal business. Discuss special needs, such as hearing or vision loss, mobility impairment, or special medical equipment. Determine how the senior can signal others in case of an emergency. Is a cell phone practical? Or a personal emergency response system that can be worn and activated to summon help?

Prepare emergency supplies of food, water, and medication. Pay attention to dexterity and hand/arm strength as you collect these supplies. You should store containers that can be opened by reduced hand strength even if there is no power. Establish some method to rotate medications through the emergency supplies so they do not expire. Include spare keys, spare eyeglasses, extra medication, a flashlight, and some extra clothing in your kit.

O—Outline the Plan in Writing

A written plan will help all involved remember what you discussed. Keep it simple and post it for easy access. Include the list of contacts and indicate next to each name the situations for which they should be contacted. Four key contacts to highlight:

1. The first person the senior would call for assistance.

2. The first family contact for members of your team to call.

3. The first person the family could contact to check on an older person.

4. The out-of-state contact

Include the list of your IN TOUCH team. Also prepare a page of medical information: conditions treated, medications and dosages, doctors, and so on. List any arrangements made for pet care. Distribute this plan to key team members.

In a separate folder, collect copies of other important information that might be needed in or immediately after an emergency. This could include insurance policies and other legal and financial information (copies only; keep originals in a safe-deposit box). Do not distribute this.

U—Update as situations change

Review the plan with key members of your team. Incorporate suggestions. Review the plan regularly and update the plan when major changes occur, such as health conditions or contact information. Update your plan at least annually. Holiday get-togethers may be a good time.

C—Communicate Regularly and Test

Check in with members of your team regularly. If you find that you are regularly unable to contact any key member, consider making a change. It may also be useful to test elements of your plan: try to make a meal or two from emergency supplies and using no electricity. Check communication tools, like cell phones. And don't forget to repeat your hazards walk-through each year to look for new hazards and to assure that smoke detectors and other safety equipment are functional.

H—Have Peace of Mind

In an emergency, stay calm and work your plan. Don't panic if everything doesn't work exactly as planned. You have enough alternatives to fall back on. And after an emergency, critically evaluate your plan: what worked? What didn't? Get input from all members of your team, update the plan, and redistribute.

Emergency preparedness:
Do one thing today.

72-HOUR KITS

Ten Key Principles of 72-Hour Kits

Hurricane Katrina (Gulf Coast, 2005), Superstorm Sandy (East Coast, 2012), the Tohoku earthquake (Japan, 2011)—all of these disasters quickly overwhelmed the ability of governments to respond to victims and underscored the principle that each person, each family, must be responsible for their own safety and response. A large disaster could cut off utilities, public services, roads, bridges, and access to stores for three days or more. Officials urge each household to prepare themselves by gathering a supply of essential items (see table at end of chapter). Follow these ten guidelines to maximize the effectiveness of your 72-hour kit.

1. The most important emergency tool is your brain. It is portable, expandable, and infinitely adaptable. Fill it with information and protect it from panic.

2. Tailor your kits to the needs of your family. Include items that are important to your family, not someone else's. Include food you'll eat, clothes you'll wear, and games your family finds fun.

3. Emergency kits don't have to be expensive. Build them now with supplies on hand and then upgrade gradually. Shop at discount stores and watch for sales.

4. Your survival supplies must be gathered into a single location before an emergency occurs. Pack contents in waterproof, nonbreakable containers. Store everything in backpacks, duffle bags, or roller suitcases. Put the kits in a convenient location that everyone knows.

5. Include multiple solutions to problems. For example: store water as well as water purification tablets. Or store battery-powered flashlights as well as chemical light sticks.

6. Plan for comfort as well as survival. Technically, you could survive on much less than you will have in your kit, but what could you add to reduce the emotional impact of a stressful situation? Adequate light, warm food, and a good night's sleep all reduce stress.

7. Your kits should be portable in case you have to evacuate on short notice. Keep a list of non-kit items you want to grab if you have time and space.

8. Don't forget Spot and Fluffy's needs.

9. If you borrow from a kit for those daily emergencies (this is allowed; an emergency is an emergency), make it a priority to replace the item. Put a list of what's in the kits in the top, to make it easier to inventory. Check and update the kits every six months. An easy time to remember is when you set the clocks back in the fall and forward in the spring. (Those are good times to change the batteries in your smoke detectors too.) Check the food, replace the water, rotate the batteries. Do the clothes still fit growing children? Is there any insect or water damage?

10. Involve everyone in getting the kits together. And involve everyone by practicing with them. If you want to know what should go in your family's survival kit, try living out of it for twenty-four hours. Or try cooking a meal without your stove. If the lights went out tonight, how would you cope? Could you entertain yourselves without TV? How much water do you use if the taps are shut off?

Only you can prepare yourself for emergencies. Preparedness is no more complicated than imagining what an emergency would be like and then doing things now that will make life easier then. A well-maintained 72-hour kit will enable you to be self-reliant in the case of an emergency.

What Should You Put in a 72-hour Kit?

The table at the end of the chapter contains a tailorable list of all the items you should consider putting in your 72-hour kit. The table is organized into four columns of lists: the bare minimum required for survival; other essential additions; items to improve your convenience level, and "luxury" items. You can tailor your own kit to your own family and your own situation and your own limits of time, space, and money. Start by gathering the items listed in the "Survival" column as a minimum. Then add the items listed in the "Essential" column. It is highly recommended that your 72-hour kits also include all or most of the "Convenience" column items. Quantities will depend on the size of your family. If you have time, room, and money, you may want to add some of the items in the "Luxury" column, although this can make the kit larger and less portable. Here are some additional tips to improve your 72-hour kits:

Overall 72-Hour Kit Tips

- Keep a copy of the list you used to assemble your kit as an inventory.

- If you use the following table, mark items that you don't want to keep with the kit but may want to grab in a real emergency if time and space allow.

- Review and update the contents of your 72-hour kit every six months, when you set the clocks back or forward for daylight savings time.

Food and Water Tips

- Include familiar foods that are tasty.

- Stress changes eating habits; try smaller servings of a variety of foods, rather than a large helping of a single dish.

- Select low-preparation foods; you won't want to cook much in an emergency.

- Store food in unbreakable, rodent-proof containers.

- Don't forget food for pets.

- Store at least one gallon of water per person per day.

- For 72-hour kit water storage, two-liter soda bottles work best; milk jugs degrade, glass breaks.

- Include water purification tablets and instructions.

- Don't store heavy items on top of water; containers could crack.

Shelter and Bedding Tips

- "Space" blankets don't take up much space. If you can afford them, buy "bivy bags" instead of blankets since they give better protection.

- Wool blankets, polypropylene, and synthetic fleeces insulate even when wet. Cotton and down do not.

- Sleeping bags are ideal for emergency kits but more expensive.

- Store foam earplugs for everyone; they may make it easier to sleep in noisy public shelters.

Clothing Tips

- Make sure clothing is sturdy, warm, large, and layerable.

- Make sure you keep up with children's growth; check every six months.

- Store shoes that have sturdy soles: disasters often leave debris and foot hazards.

- Include knit caps and knit gloves or mittens.

- In cold or even cool weather, getting wet can lead to hypothermia. Rain gear could be lifesaving: large garbage bags work as ponchos in a pinch.

- Include a small sewing kit with safety pins in case you have to repair or adapt clothes.

Light/Heat Tips

- A flashlight with fresh batteries and extra bulb is essential. LED flashlights are inexpensive, powerful, and stingy with batteries. When in doubt, get extra ones.

- A strap-on headlamp will give you the ability to do tasks that require two hands. A battery lantern will light a space best (LED models are widely available).

- Flashlights that take standard batteries are the simplest.

- Candles or flame lanterns do not store well (especially in warm garages or trunks) or transport well and can create additional fire hazards.

- Charcoal (takes up lots of room), solid-fuel emergency stove, or backpacker's stove (may require special canisters or liquid fuel) can be used for cooking. Don't forget matches.

Safety note: Do not use open flames until you are sure there are no gas leaks. Ventilate adequately. Never leave an open flame unattended, and keep children away. NEVER cook indoors with charcoal; carbon monoxide is deadly.

First-Aid Tips

- A good first-aid manual is a must.
- The major objective of a 72-hour first-aid kit is to treat minor injuries and prevent infections: include antiseptic pads, anti-bacterial ointment, and adhesive bandages.
- Match the contents of your first-aid kit with your knowledge level.
- Include aspirin, acetaminophen, or ibuprofen for pain relief.
- Add antihistamines for allergic reactions, stuffy noses, and nausea.
- Large sterile dressings, gauze rolls (get plenty), tape, and elastic bandages can be used for larger, more serious injuries.
- A bandanna has many uses in first aid and in general. Include a few.
- Don't forget scissors, tweezers, and a needle.
- Latex gloves can prevent the spread of germs.

Sanitation Tips

- Hand sanitizer is quick and convenient, but it has a limited shelf life. Double-bag it to minimize leaking. Moist towelettes are convenient and versatile. If they dry out, add a little bit of water to rehydrate. Include some hand soap as well; double-bag it.
- Paper towels come in handy.
- A five-gallon bucket with plastic sacks/ties and some disinfectant can make an improvised toilet.
- Don't forget toilet paper.
- Each person will want a personal comfort kit: toothbrush/paste, hand towel, soap, comb, and so on.
- Remember diapers and feminine hygiene products.
- Extra zipper plastic sacks and garbage bags have a variety of uses.

Communication Tips

- A battery-powered radio and some batteries are essential for keeping current on the situation. There are reliable models that include solar and crank-powered options. Some will even recharge a cell phone by crank power.

- Include a paper list of key contacts and phone numbers. The electronic directories we have on our phones are useless when the battery dies.

- Include a pencil and some paper in case you want to leave messages for someone or keep notes of things you learn.

- Recent photos of family members can be a morale booster and can help officials locate missing persons more quickly.

Personal/Valuables Tips

- Many emergencies will render ATMs and credit cards inoperative. Cash will be needed if any purchases can be made: store small bills and coins.

- Don't forget personal medications (ask a pharmacist about storability). Depending on your medication, you might need to rotate a fresh supply every month.

- Include copies of important papers. The originals should be kept in a secure place.

- Include extra glasses, denture supplies, elderly or infant needs, extra pacifiers, and so on.

Utensils/Tools Tips

- A sharp pocketknife is vital.

- Disposable dishes can conserve water as well as make clean-up easy.

- Include a cooking pan, pot holders, and cooking/serving utensils if you plan on cooking.

- Don't forget a can opener if you've stored canned goods. Army surplus stores sell small can openers that will store anywhere. Get a couple of them and tie them on lanyards; they are easily lost.

- Leather gloves protect hands while working or cooking.

- Versatile additions: nylon rope, duct tape, aluminum foil.

Morale Tips

- Hard candy stores well.

- Toys, games, and puzzles will keep kids busy; pack a game kit; include instructions.

- Don't pack a high-density book; pack magazines, word/number games, short story collections, and easy reads.

Emergency preparedness:
Do one thing today.

How to use these tables: Put together a 72-hour kit to meet your own needs and fit your own time/space/money limits. Start by gathering the items listed in the "Survival" column as a minimum. Then add the items listed in the "Essential" column. I highly recommended that your 72-hour kits also include all or most of the "Convenience" column items (next page). Quantities will depend on the size of family. If you have time, money, and room, you may want to add some of the items in the "luxury" column, although this makes the kit quite a bit larger and much less portable.

Category	Survival Minimum	Essential Additions
1. Food/Water	Food, none (adult) Water: 2 c/day: 2 qt/person Water purification & instructions	Food, any (unbreakable packages) Water: 1 gal/person per day
2. Shelter/Bedding	Space blanket	Space or bivy bag Umbrella
3. Clothing	30 gal garbage sacks 1 gal, 1 qt plastic bags (plain not zip)	Warm, layers (fleece/wool) Wool cap Warm, dry, sturdy footwear
4. Heat/Light	Matches (waterproof)	Flashlight w/batteries Cooking heat (sterno or solid fuel)
5. First Aid	Basic kit First-aid manual Bandanna	
6. Sanitation	Hand sanitizer (double bagged)	Toilet paper Trowel Plastic bags, ties Soap (hand/dish) Feminine hygiene Diapers (if needed) Moist towelettes
7. Communication	Card w/phone numbers	Contact plan Family pictures w/names Extra phone charger cable
8. Personal/Valuable	Personal medication (rotate)	Cash: small bills and coins
9. Tools/Utensils	Sharp pocket knife Functional container or pack for kit	Paper cups, plates Plastic forks, spoons Aluminum foil Paper towels Rope/cord/string
10. Morale		Radio w/batteries Dust masks

Category	Convenience Additions	Luxury Additions
1. Food/Water	Food ready-to-eat Water: 5–10 gal/person Pet food Special diet foods	Luxury foods Water: 50–100 gal/family Salt, sugar, spices Multiple purification methods
2. Shelter/Bedding	Ground cloth (sheet plastic) Blankets (wool or fleece) Earplugs (foam, for public shelter)	Tent, trailer Sleeping bags Closed cell foam pads
3. Clothing	Rain jacket/pants Extra socks, underwear Gloves	Complete change of clothes Sewing kit, shoelaces, safety pins Laundry soap
4. Heat/Light	LED headlamp w/batteries Flint and steel Hiker's stove/fuel	Multiple fuel source Emergency generator Battery lantern Camp stove w/fuel Space heater w/fuel
5. First Aid	Expanded kit	EMT kit Fire extinguisher (ABC) Insect repellent, sunscreen
6. Sanitation	Plastic bucket w/tight lid Large plastic bags Toilet seat Disinfectant, bleach Hand towel, cloth Toothbrush, paste, floss Paper towels	Port-a-potty Newspaper Deodorant Shampoo Shaving kit Nail clippers Comb, brush
7. Communication	Whistles Paper and pencil (not pen)	Flares, light sticks Map, compass
8. Personal/Valuable	Copies of important papers Valuables Watch/clock	Mirror (metal) Infant/elderly needs Sunglasses, extra glasses
9. Tools/Utensils	Manual can opener Skillet, lid Cook pot, lid Gloves, leather Steel wool, pot scrubber Hot pads Extra plastic sacks (small)	Crescent wrench Screwdrivers Pliers, scissors Baling wire, duct tape Solar still Shovel Axe, saw, whetstone Crowbar, hammer
10. Morale	Hard candy Toys, games, puzzles Paper, crayons Emergency survival book	Journal, pencil (not pen) Hobbies, crafts Magazines, books

EVACUATION PLANNING

What Do You Take? Where Do You Go?

The key lesson from Hurricane Katrina was the same key lesson from Superstorm Sandy, which was also the same key lesson from the Tohoku earthquake: get out when authorities (or your own good sense) tell you to get out. Maybe even before they tell you. This lesson is the one that will preserve your lives. Throughout the year, we hear of events and calamities requiring people—sometimes few, sometimes many— to leave their homes. Evacuations can be forced by rising waters and flooding; they can be caused by chemical spills or releases; they can be caused by wildfire. Nearly every year, Gulf and Atlantic Coast residents are forced to leave their homes as hurricanes threaten to come ashore, with associated storm surge. Some parts of the world are threatened by volcanic activity, lava flows, mud slides, and ash fall. Even a house fire causes an evacuation of one family.

Evacuations can last hours or, less frequently, days. After Katrina, they lasted for months, and some of the residents just plain relocated. Most of us have never been required to evacuate. In the case of disaster or emergency, when should you evacuate? Where would you go? What should you take? What should you expect?

When to Evacuate

Leave when you are in danger. Thousands of lives were saved on 9/11 because people evacuated when they were told to or when they saw the danger. In many cases, you won't be able to make that determination by yourself because you don't have access to all of the critical information. You may not be aware of a chemical spill. You won't be able to predict a river's peak or a storm's path. In these situations, you should leave when authorities tell you to. Authorities will use public communications (TV, radio) when they have enough time. In short notice situations, they may use vehicle-mounted public broadcast systems and even door-to-door notification if necessary. In the case of storms and hurricanes, forecasters can give a day or two of notice. Sometimes potential evacuees are given hours of notice. In New Jersey in 2012, a railroad bridge failed, dumping several rail tankers full of chemicals into the water. The closest neighbors had no warning and were out of their houses for several days. In cases like this, evacuees will only have a minute or two to grab family members—and maybe a well-placed 72-hour kit—and go.

The most important thing is to get your family to safety, but if you have time, here are some additional actions you might take:

- Don't panic.

- Gather essential items. A possible list is described later in this chapter.

- Secure your house. In hurricanes that means boarding up windows. In floods it means putting furniture and valuables on upper floors. In a chemical spill it might mean closing the windows, vents, and air intakes. Disconnect utilities if told to. Take actions to prevent freezing pipes if weather is a problem.

- Put on sturdy and practical clothes, especially shoes.

- Let others know where you are going. Call your out-of-state contact.

- Make provisions for your pets if you plan on going to a public shelter—many shelters do not accept pets for health and control reasons.

Where to Go

When authorities direct an evacuation, they may also determine a safe evacuation route for you to follow. Traffic is likely to be heavy and slow. Be extra patient and extra courteous: all those around you will be just as disoriented as you, maybe more. Don't take shortcuts.

Stay on recommended routes to avoid being trapped by unexpected road closures or running into a drifting chemical cloud. Follow all traffic regulations: an accident in an emergency situation is doubly dangerous, and emergency services may be tied up elsewhere.

You may already have determined in your family emergency plan where you will go and how you will contact each other in an evacuation emergency. Each family should have at least three evacuation locations determined in advance:

1. A safe place outside of the home where you can gather if you need to escape a burning house. When you have fire and exit drills, be sure to practice going to this spot.

2. A friend or family member's house outside of the immediate neighborhood but close enough to walk to, where you could go in a localized evacuation.

3. A friend or family member's house outside of the community for larger evacuations, like hurricanes. Also, check the school emergency plan to make sure that you know where your schoolchildren will be sent if they are required to evacuate their schools.

If you cannot get to one of these family plan locations, then public shelters—set up and run by the Red Cross or other community service organizations—are a possible solution. If authorities don't direct you to a public shelter, the radio may broadcast shelter locations you can go to. In the absence of other information, check public buildings—schools, municipal buildings, and churches—since these are the most likely places for shelters to be established.

Once you get to your temporary location—wherever it is—check in with your out-of-state contact. Having someone outside of the area or state gives you a single checkpoint for all your family to report their status. This will help you exchange information to reunite in the event that everyone did not make it immediately to the planned gathering spot. Designate your out-of-state contact, make it part of your family plan, and make sure that everyone in the family memorizes the number and carries a copy of it with them.

What to Take

- 72-hour kits. One of the reasons 72-hour kits must be pre-gathered—and not just a list of stuff you have somewhere in your house—is that you may need to grab them at a moment's notice and evacuate with them. Shelters may not have everything you need or want to have. They provide protection from the elements and may supply food and water.

Here are some other things you may want to bring for your own comfort:

- First-aid supplies for minor injuries
- Personal medications, including prescriptions
- Extra clothes
- A child's favorite toy
- A battery-powered radio
- Quiet entertainment, books or games, paper and pencil
- A recent picture of each member of your family, to help locate them
- List of phone numbers: family, neighbors, places where family members might go
- Earplugs: it may be difficult to sleep in a shelter without them
- Cash in small denominations
- Important papers: financial and investment, insurance, household inventory, deeds, wills
- Your own personal hygiene items
- Car resources. Since you will likely evacuate in your car, don't forget all of the resources you may have available in your car too. It's a good idea to keep your car on the full side of the gas tank.
- Some things not to take: panic, alcoholic beverages, firearms

What to Expect

Each shelter situation will be different, but in general you might expect the following:

- Expect to sign in and to receive instructions from shelter managers. Following directions will reduce the confusion level.
- Don't expect all of the conveniences of home.
- Don't expect all of the privacy or quiet or order of home. Be patient.
- Expect information from time to time about what's going on and when you can expect to go home.

- Expect to be responsible for your own hygiene. Be as sanitary as you can—wash your hands often. Be especially careful with food storage and preparations.

- Expect food and water, but don't expect a huge variety of gourmet selections. Eat as balanced a diet as you can. Drink lots of water—at least a quart a day or more, if available.

- Expect to do your part to keep improvised toilets clean and sanitary.

- Do not expect smoking to be allowed in shelters. Be considerate if you must smoke.

- Expect to be responsible for your own children. Keep them under control—improvise games to keep them occupied.

- Expect to be responsible for shelter safety and security.

- Expect to be patient. Shelter volunteers do the best they can under difficult circumstances. Give them a break and let the little things go.

Returning Home

When returning home, remember: safety first. Do not enter a damaged structure until authorities determine it's safe. Take pictures and keep careful, thorough records of any damage and/or repair costs for your insurance agent.

Wear appropriate safety gear: heavy shoes, gloves, and safety glasses. Follow instructions from authorities. Be meticulous and thorough if decontamination procedures are recommended.

Check for gas leaks. Have the gas company restore gas service if shut off or damaged. Restore utilities carefully only after checking for broken pipes, exposed wires, or other damage. Clean up hazardous chemicals or medicines that may have spilled, as well as broken glass and other hazards. Beware of exhaustion. Pace yourself and get plenty of rest. Wash your hands often. Don't drink the water until authorities declare it safe. Throw out spoiled or suspect food.

• • •

Use the guidelines here to get ready for an evacuation. Then, if evacuation is ever required, don't panic. Roll with the punches, be resourceful, be patient. Your preparation now will make it easier for you to protect your family by getting out of harm's way at a moment's notice.

Emergency preparedness:
Do one thing today.

FIRST AID

Learn First-Aid Skills and Make a Kit

Injuries are a potential component of any emergency situation. The more widespread the emergency, the greater the chances that you may have to deal with injuries to yourself or your family before help can arrive. Certainly if you have life-threatening or serious medical emergencies, you should try to get help or get to a facility, but in many cases, the emergency medical system may be too overwhelmed to get to the less-serious injuries quickly. Although no one expects you to be an ER physician, learning several things and having certain supplies on hand will improve your effectiveness in a medical emergency.

Learn First Aid

Take a course. If you've never had a first-aid class, now is the time to find one and sign up. The Red Cross teaches first aid, as do some community education programs, fire or police stations, community colleges, and workplaces. You will learn how to assess a victim for life-threatening conditions; clear airways, check for breathing and circulation, and administer cardiopulmonary resuscitation (CPR); recognize and treat shock; treat internal and external bleeding; treat burns; treat broken bones, sprains, and dislocations; treat injuries from extreme heat and cold; and treat bites, stings, and poisonings. Even if you have had first-aid training in the past, it pays to update your knowledge on this ever-expanding topic.

Get a good first-aid reference book that tells you how to recognize and treat various medical emergencies. Some hospitals or urgent care centers distribute emergency handbooks for glove compartments or households. Most commercially prepared first-aid kits will also have a handbook. Although your first response to an emergency usually won't give you time to consult a handbook, there is usually some point where you will be able to review the proper section of the handbook to make sure you've done all you can. The handbook is also a good review resource when you want to brush up on your skills.

Prepare a First-Aid Kit

What goes into your first-aid kit depends on what emergencies you expect and what first-aid skills you have. For example, someone with medical training might include a suture kit for sewing up wounds. Some lesser-trained people might be uncomfortable with the idea of sutures or IVs.

Your home kit (wide range and smaller injuries) will be different than a commuter's (auto accident trauma) or a backpacker's (personal injuries far from help). Although some good pre-packaged first-aid kits are available, you will be better off if you create your own kit. Then you won't pay for items that you will never use, and you can add items that you know you frequently use. Best of all, if you build the kit, you know what is in it. Whether you buy it or build it, keep a list of the items you have in the kit to make updating and replenishing easier. Most kits will include the following:

- First-aid manual
- Over-the-counter pain medication, like aspirin, acetaminophen, or ibuprofen (the most used item of my own kit)
- Antihistamine tablets to reduce the allergic reaction to stings and bites (if you have severe allergic reactions, see a doctor about portable epinephrine injection devices)
- Latex rubber gloves to wear when giving first aid
- Rescue breather for giving CPR
- Hand sanitizer, antiseptic wipes; alcohol or iodine, for cleaning your hands as well as wounds
- Small plastic syringe for irrigating cuts and scrapes

- Antibiotic gel or cream to put on cuts and scrapes
- Assorted adhesive bandages—medium, large, and butterfly type
- Assorted gauze dressings ($2'' \times 2''$, $3'' \times 3''$, $4'' \times 4''$)
- Assorted width gauze roller bandages ($2''$ and $3''$)
- Ace elastic bandage
- Bandage tape
- Pressure bandages (diapers, nursing pads, feminine hygiene pads all could be used here)
- Bandannas have many uses, from pressure dressings to splint ties and slings
- Cold packs are useful for reducing swelling or treating painful burns
- Safety scissors are useful for cutting bandages and removing clothing
- Needle and tweezers are handy for removing splinters and stingers
- Sterile eyewash
- Safety pins have uses in securing wraps and slings
- Some people also store splints, but usually you can find all sorts of things to improvise with. In many cases, you don't need to splint at all—you only need to immobilize until help comes.

Practice First-Aid Principles in Emergencies

- Don't panic. Take a deep breath and remind yourself that you know some things that might help. Your confidence will be contagious.
- Make sure the scene is safe, and avoid becoming another victim.
- Always summon help first in a medical emergency. When in doubt, call. If the emergency turns out to be less serious than you thought, you can send them home. If it is serious, they will arrive that much faster.
- Treat the victim where you find them; don't move them unless the scene is not safe.
- The first priorities are usually to assure the victim has a clear airway, is breathing, and has circulation. If the victim is conscious, these

things are present. If these things are not present, apply the techniques you've learned in your CPR course.

- Bleeding from even minor injuries can look worse than it is, so don't panic: stop bleeding with direct pressure over the wound. First-aid courses will teach you the tools and the techniques.

- In all emergency situations, even small ones, assume the victim is in shock or will go into shock, and treat them as you were taught in your first-aid course: keep them comfortable and warm.

• • •

A well-rounded emergency preparedness plan includes training and equipment for first aid. Like all emergency preparedness, you may never have to use it. But then again, someone you love may need you to know it.

Emotional First Aid

In any emergency, physical safety and first aid are immediate and pressing concerns. But emergencies are also stressful and psychologically traumatic; first aid for the emotions may be required. Children often have unique emotional needs in an emergency.

Preparation Minimizes Emotional Trauma

Preparation is the first step in reducing the psychological impact of a disaster. Children can and should be involved in emergency preparedness. A key consideration is that emergency preparedness should be an ongoing activity. If you only occasionally discuss preparedness by emphasizing all the things that can go wrong and then don't take any steps to prepare, you may scare children into being afraid of everything. With emergency preparedness as an ongoing activity, however, children see that there are some dangers, and they also participate in mitigation efforts and see that the risks become less.

Some Ways to Involve Children

- Teach children common danger signals: the sound of the smoke alarm, the smell of smoke, the smell of natural gas.

- Even young children can be taught to use 911. All children should be taught their name, age, address, and parents' full names as early as possible.

- Children should be taught how to call the out-of-state contact, even from a pay phone.

- Children can understand basic principles such as staying calm, assessing the situation, escaping if required, and reporting emergencies. All children should know safe places to go (neighbors' houses and so on) if they must leave the home.

- Children should know basic street safety principles such as staying in groups, not talking to or taking anything from strangers, noticing suspicious cars, writing down license plate numbers, how to react if threatened, safe places to run, and so on.

- Teach fire safety and fire response. Practice fire escapes.

- Involve them in home hazard hunts. Make it a game to see who can spot the most hazards and then involve children in fixing them.

- Children can learn safe locations to go in case of earthquakes or tornadoes.

- Involve children in emergency practices as well as routine maintenance.

Short-Term Emotional Response—Stay Calm and Listen

If you stay calm, those around you will stay calmer. No situation gets better with panic. Your calm influence will go a long way toward reassuring children (and other adults). Be honest. Only say what you know about the emergency. Do not speculate. Do not lie. Don't make promises you can't keep.

Listen to the upset individual. Realize their feelings are real feelings. Do not dismiss or make light of them. Discuss them one at a time. Listen. Really listen—don't interrupt. Give them your attention; give them eye contact. Do not argue or use force.

Provide warm, nourishing food and encourage rest when possible. Most obstacles look smaller when your stomach is full and you are rested. Do not administer drugs unless under a doctor's supervision.

Typical fears of children after a disaster include fear of recurrence, fear of separation from family, and fear of being left alone. Reunite children with their families as soon as possible. If the family is already together, keep it together as much as possible. Try not to leave children in a "safe place" while you go off to survey the damage.

Listen to children express their fears, even if they aren't rational. Listen to their version of the event. Encourage children to talk. Reassure them with words as well as actions—let them know that you will take care of them. Let them know it's okay to be afraid. Gently help them to realize many of their fears are unlikely. Speak to children at their level, both physically and mentally. Don't speak down to them, but put the situation in words they can understand. If appropriate, use reassuring physical contact.

Long-Term Emotional Response—Be Patient and Listen

Keep listening with patience. You may have to listen to the same stories and the same fears and give the same reassurances over and over again. Also, resume normal routines as soon as possible. Routines are comforting and reassuring. Include children in age-appropriate cleanup actions. Be understanding but be firm in retaining control over family activities. Avoid being overly permissive about getting back to normal routines. If there is difficulty at bedtime, parents and children should agree on the day for the child to return to his own bed and then stick with it. Be firm, but avoid spanking or shouting to enforce your expectations.

Some effects may last for a while. There may be depression, insomnia, nightmares, anger, or incorrigibility. Many of these effects will dissipate with time and care, but some may need professional help. Realize your role—you cannot be all things to all people. You may not have proper training. You may not have unlimited time or energy to devote. You may need to seek professional assistance on behalf of the victim. Realize that this is not a sign of failure but is a mature and loving response to speed the recovery of the victim. Don't be afraid to seek professional help for emotional problems when you don't know what to do. Professionals are trained to identify specific emotional conditions and are experienced in providing appropriate responses that lead the victim to resolution. You should call professionals

- any time you don't feel capable of responding to the victim's needs

- when your patience wears out

- when aggressive behavior or regressive behavior persists beyond a few days

- when fears and irrational anxiety increase rather than diminish

Start with a call to your pediatrician or family physician. In many cases, advice can be given over the phone. In some cases, an interview will be requested. Some regressive behavior like bed-wetting, thumb-sucking, or clinging can be normal but should only last for a few days. Focus on reassurance and positive reinforcement to overcome the behavior.

All emergencies, whether specific to your family or widespread, will produce a range of normal emotional reactions. Preparation can reduce the extent of negative reactions; calmness and patience are the best tools for responding to them.

Emergency preparedness:
Do one thing today.

First-Aid Kit Supplies

Item	Use	Include in these kits:		
		Home Kit	Car Kit	Pocket Kit
First-Aid Manual	Remind yourself of what you learned in class	Yes	Yes	Optional
Bandages				
Adhesive strips, various sizes	Dress small injuries, cuts scrapes, bites; prevent infection. This is the most used part of most kits.	100 total	20 total	5–10 total
Sterile dressings:				
2x2, 3x3, 4x4	Dress larger wounds, scrapes, burns, etc.	4–6 total	10 total	2 total
5x9, 8x10	Dress very large wounds, scrapes, burns, etc.	2 each	2 each	
Gauze rolls:				
2″, 4″	Hold dressings in place	3 each	3 each	
Tape, 1″, 2″	Hold dressings in place, temporarily close wounds	1 each	2, 2″	1, 1″
Pressure pads	Apply pressure to bleeding wound	4–6	10	
Elastic roller wrap, 3″	Hold dressings in place, provide support to joints	2–3	2–3	1
Bandanna	Dressing, sling, pressure, washcloth, towel, etc.	1–2	2–3	1
Medicines				
Acetaminophen or Ibuprophen	Pain relief, inflammation reduction; include children's doses— follow instructions	100 ct	10 ct	10 ct
Antihistamines	Allergic reaction treatment	4–8 ct	4–8 ct	4–8 ct
Antiseptic wipes	Cleanse small wounds, wash hands	10 pks	10 pks	5 pks
Antibiotic gel	Protect small injuries from infection	1 large	1 small	1 small
Ipecac syrup	Induce vomiting in some poisoning cases	1 bottle		
Sterile eyewash	Cleanse foreign material or chemicals from eye	1 bottle	1 bottle	
Burn gel	Treat small burns	10 sm pk		1 sm pk
Calamine lotion	Treat bites, poison ivy, nettles, etc.	1		1 sm pk

First-Aid Kit Supplies (continued)

Item	Use	Include in these kits:		
		Home Kit	Car Kit	Pocket Kit
Tools				
Rubber gloves	Minimize risk from infection, blood-borne pathogens	10 pr	5 pr	1 pr
Rescue breather	Minimize risk from infection, blood-borne pathogens	1	1	1
EMT shears	Remove obstructing clothing, seat belts, etc.	1	1	1
Irrigation syringe	Irrigate wounds to remove foreign materials	1		
Splints, small to large	Immobilize broken bones, injured joints	various	various	
Cold packs	Reduce swelling, reduce burn pain	2–3	1–2	
Needle/tweezers	Remove splinters, quills, etc.; treat blisters	1 each	1 each	1 each
Flashlight	Provide aid in dark; look in throats, ears	1 w/batt	1 w/batt	
Thermometer	Measure temperature	1		
Other				
Water bottle	wash wounds	1 bott	1–2 bott	
Cotton swabs	Apply medications	20–50		2–5
Safety pins	Hold bandages/slings in place, repair clothing	5–10	5–10	2–3
Moleskin	Prevent/cushion blisters on feet while hiking	1 sht		½ sht
Nail clippers	Trim hiker's toenails; treat hang-nails, etc.	1		1
Space blanket	Provide warmth, treat shock	2	2	1
Matches, waterproof	Sterilize needles, tweezers; start fire	25–50	25–50	25–50
Plastic bags	Various	5 various	10 var	1–3
Paper and pencil	Send information, instructions; make notes	1 each	1 each	1 each

WATER STORAGE

Emergency Water Storage Q&A

Q: How much water should I store?

A: Although basic survival is possible on less, store about one gallon per person per day. Additional water could be used for things like sponge baths, flushing the toilet, and "survival laundry." Most authorities agree that you shouldn't try to store more than a two-week supply.

Family of	Minimum Supply	"Luxury" Supply
1	14 gallons	28 gallons
2	28 gallons	56 gallons
3	42 gallons	84 gallons
4	56 gallons	112 gallons
5	70 gallons	140 gallons
6	84 gallons	168 gallons
7	90 gallons	196 gallons

Q: What types of containers should I use?

A: You have several choices, each with advantages and disadvantages.

- **Glass:** If you use containers smaller than one gallon, you will have too many to worry about. No glass containers larger than a gallon are likely to be available. Glass can be sterilized, but it breaks easily (like in earthquakes).

- **Metal**: must be of a suitable alloy (stainless steel) or appropriately lined (polyethylene) and will be expensive.

- **Plastic**: The best solution for bulk storage is the HDPE barrel. They come in fifteen-gallon, thirty-gallon, and fifty-five-gallon sizes and can be purchased new or used as soft drink syrup barrels. If you go with used, be sure that only food products have been stored. They must be thoroughly washed and repeatedly rinsed (the local car wash has high-pressure water), but they make an efficient way to store large quantities of water. Avoid milk jugs. Two-liter soda containers are made of less porous PET plastic and will clean better and last longer than milk jugs. Two-liter bottles are light and portable but are also flimsy and awkward to carry. Another kind of storage container is the mylar bladder in a cardboard box. These are more expensive (three to five dollars per five-gallon box), but they are square and store more easily than other containers. Be careful not to stack too high or the lower boxes could be crushed and collapse.

Never store drinking water in containers that have been used for petroleum products or other chemicals; they are impossible to clean and will certainly leach contaminants into the water.

Keeping some five-gallon containers handy is useful; in a long-term disruption of water service, relief agencies will likely bring water trucks to a central neighborhood location, and the smaller containers are more portable than the barrels.

Q: How can I get water out of a large drum?

A: Hand pumps made especially for large drums are available at emergency preparedness stores. You can also use a simple siphon made from a clean rubber tube or garden hose. Instead of sucking on the hose, fill it with water to get it started. If you store the drum slightly above the ground (on pallets or two-by-fours), you can even siphon the last bit without wrestling the container.

Q: Why shouldn't I use plastic milk jugs to store water?

A: The plastic is not formulated for long-term use and will degrade over several months' time. Also, high porosity makes it impossible to clean and allows odor/taste pickup from the storage area.

Q: Where should I keep my stored water?

A: Water weighs about eight pounds per gallon; a fifty-five-gallon barrel will weigh over four hundred pounds. The larger the container, the less mobile it will be. If you choose a large-capacity container, you may still want to have a few smaller, lighter bottles around in case you need to evacuate. Always store heavy items like water bottles on lower shelves if not on the floor. If you have glass containers, cushion between the bottles with cardboard; glass rattling against glass in an earthquake could create quite a mess. Store water out of sunlight, which can stimulate bacterial growth and affect plastic. Store it at a cool temperature, which will also retard bacterial growth. Some authorities recommend keeping part of your water in the basement and part in the garage in case quake damage makes it difficult to get to one or the other. Do not store plastic containers near fuels, pesticides, herbicides, and so on because all plastics are porous to some degree, and contamination could be a problem. If you store the water where it might freeze, leave several inches of headspace in the container to allow for expansion.

Q: Do I need to purify water when I put it in containers?

A: Your own culinary water is usually quite clean, and chlorinated tap water should not need additional treatment, but sometimes the container can have residual bugs. The Centers for Disease Control and Prevention (CDC) recommend purifying water with eight drops (⅛ teaspoon) of fresh (less than one year old), unscented liquid bleach (4–6 percent sodium hypochlorite) per gallon. A quarter teaspoon or sixteen drops should be used if the water is cloudy.

Q: How often should I replace my stored water?

A: Experts differ on how often—if ever—to replace your water. You can check it frequently for smell and taste and replace it as needed. I try to empty and refill our containers about twice a year.

Q: Do I need to purify the water again when I take it from the container?

A: Only you can tell when you inspect the water. Clean water should be clear without any odor, unless there is a leftover chlorine smell from the purification. If you smell any questionable odors or see any growth in the containers, purify the water. In fact, if you have any question at all, purify.

Emergency Water Purification

There are many sources of water in an emergency, but most require purification before use.

Water Sources

- **Stored Water**: The most reliable source of water will be whatever you store. Experts recommend storing about one gallon per person per day for up to two weeks.

- **House system**: Water heaters and supply pipes contain from thirty to sixty gallons of water. To protect this water from being contaminated or siphoned out of your system, shut the main water valve into your house immediately after an emergency. If there is a reasonable chance that the water main has become contaminated, then the water heater and house pipes will also be affected if water flows through them after the emergency. If there is any doubt about safety, treat the water. Also, turn off the gas to the water heater if you are going to empty the water without refilling it.

- **Toilets**: Toilet tanks (*not* the bowls) can be sources of drinking water *only* if they do not contain a colored disinfectant. Always purify.

- **Water Beds**: *Not* safe for drinking. The plastic used for the mattress was probably treated with fungicides or bactericides and may leach toxins into the water. Most of us have also added chemical treatments to the water, which makes it unsuitable for human consumption. Do not count on this water for any purpose except non-drinkable sanitation uses, flushing toilets, and so on.

- **Swimming Pools/Spas**: *Not* safe for drinking. Because of the chemicals used to purify and balance the pH, swimming pools and hot tubs build up salts that can damage the kidneys if the water is used for drinking. Do not count on this water for any purpose except non-drinkable sanitation uses.

- **Surface water**: This source includes rivers, canals, lakes, ponds, and other standing water. Surface water should always be purified.

- **Ground water**: Access to this water requires a well. If there is any doubt about its safety, treat the water.

Water Purification Methods

A number of elements can make water unsafe:

- Parasites, the most infamous of which are giardia and cryptosporidium

- Bacteria including strep, staph, salmonella, E. coli, and pneumonia

- Viruses (rare)

- Pollutants including fertilizers, pesticides, and petroleum products

If the water looks, smells, or tastes odd, or comes from a questionable source, purify it. Any time your water source is open or outdoors—no matter how clean the water "looks"—you need to purify. There are three main methods of purification: boiling, chemical treatment, and filtering.

Boiling

Water can be disinfected by bringing to a rolling boil. The CDC recommends boiling the water for one minute at sea level, three minutes over an altitude of six thousand five hundred feet.

Chemical Treatment

- **Chlorine:** Household bleach that contains 4–6 percent sodium hypochlorite (check the label) can be added to clear water at the rate of two drops per quart (eight drops or ⅛ teaspoon per gallon) for clear water and four drops per quart (sixteen drops or ¼ teaspoon per gallon) for cloudy water, and allowing to stand for 30 minutes. Use newer bleach, since the strength of bleach weakens with time. Double the treatment for bleach that is over a year old; do not use bleach that is over two years old. A slight chlorine odor should be detectable after treatment. If not, repeat the treatment. Liquid bleach treatment may not be fully effective against cryptosporidium. Halazone tablets are a solid form of the same treatment and should be used according to manufacturer's instructions. Halazone, however, does not store for long periods and loses most of its strength in days after the package is opened. If you buy extra bleach to have on hand for purification, be sure to store it out of reach of children, and make sure it cannot fall and split open in an earthquake.

- **Iodine**: This comes in commercial tablet form (Potable Aqua, and so on). Pay close attention to the expiration date; older tablets lose their strength. Buy small quantities (store out of reach of children) more frequently and keep your supply fresh. Follow manufacturer's instructions for storage, dosage, and "contact time," the time you let the water sit before drinking. Also, treated water takes on a taste that some find objectionable. Ascorbic acid (vitamin C) helps, and powdered drink flavorings may make the water palatable.

Safety note: Pregnant women and people with thyroid problems should not ingest iodine.

Filtering

Here we're talking about filters specifically designed to purify water. Your water softener, for example, can remove minerals and suspended solids so the water tastes better, but it cannot make water safer to drink. The same thing is true for many under-the-sink or faucet-end filters. Water-purifying filters work on the principle that if you pump the water through holes smaller than the microorganisms, the bugs will stay behind. Some filters additionally flow the water through a bed of iodine compound or silver nanoparticles to kill bioagents. Most models also come with carbon filters that remove organic chemicals and tastes. These filters are remarkably effective, although the output is usually measured in pints per minute.

The main drawback to portable filters is cost. Although you can find cheap copies of the reputable devices, this is not a piece of equipment you want to scrimp on; buy the best you can afford. You can purchase reverse osmosis filters or microstraining filters that rely on pore size to remove germs and cysts like cryptosporidium and giardia. Look for a certification that the filter has been tested and certified by NSF Standard 53 or Standard 58 for cyst removal.

Magazines with an outdoor theme such as *Backpacker* or *Outside* frequently review and evaluate equipment like this. Look for these filters at outdoor equipment or emergency preparedness stores.

● ● ●

Any of these methods is adequate to produce safe drinking water, but if you have no way to purify water, you should carefully weigh the possible hazards of drinking untreated water against the obvious need to sustain life. Antibiotics are available to combat giardia, for example, if you need to drink untreated water to stay alive. Remember, the purpose of preparedness is to give you and your family the greatest odds of getting out of an emergency situation with the least harm.

Emergency preparedness:
Do one thing today.

LONG-TERM FOOD STORAGE

Food Storage Key Principles

For many, "emergency preparedness" is synonymous with "food storage." In addition to emergency preparedness, though, there are many practical reasons to store food:

- Buying in bulk can be cheaper than day-to-day shopping.

- Fewer trips to the store means less impulse buying.

- Food on hand gives you options for those "what should we have for dinner?" nights.

- By preserving your own produce, you control the quality and content.

- Stored food provides a cushion, allowing your family to weather financial crises like unemployment or unexpected financial burden.

Food storage, however, is more than buying wheat in nitrogen-packed buckets and putting it in the basement. Here are four key principles of food storage.

1. Store What You Eat

If you don't store what you regularly use, you will throw it away in a few years. If you don't store what you use, you will unnecessarily increase the stress of an emergency by having to fix and eat completely different foods. If you don't store what you will use, your body may not adapt well to food (like whole wheat) that you have to eat in an emergency.

Here is a simple process for deciding what to store if you want to have a year's worth of food. Families eats the same ten to twenty meals about 80–90 percent of the time. These are the meals we fix so often that we almost don't need to look at recipes to whip them up. You probably could list them right now, with a little thought. Or you could post a piece of paper on the refrigerator and keep track for about a month. Write down main dishes and add side dishes to make a nutritionally balanced diet.

Once you have a list of meals, write down next to each meal the required ingredients. You'll find that you use similar ingredients—tomato sauce, for instance—for different meals. Also note what items you use regularly, like spices, because you'll need a supply of staples on hand too. Compile this information on a single table by listing meals down the left side and ingredients across the top. When you have filled ingredient quantities for all the meals in the table, sum each ingredient at the bottom. For example, in the twenty meals you have identified, if four of them require two cans each of tomato sauce, then the sum for tomato sauce would be eight cans. Do the same for each ingredient.

Now count the number of meals you have identified and divide into 365 to calculate how many times you would have to eat each meal in a year. For example, if you identified fifteen meals, you would have to eat each one twenty-five times (round any fraction up) in a year. If you have identified twenty meals, you would eat each one nineteen times, and so on. Multiply this number by each of your ingredients to calculate how much of each you would need to prepare your meal list for an entire year. For example, say you came up with fifteen meals and the sum for tomato sauce to fix all those meals once is eight cans. Since you'll need to fix each meal twenty-five times in a year, multiply eight cans by twenty-five times and you'll find that you need two hundred cans of tomato sauce for a year's meals. Do this for each ingredient, and do the same for breakfast and lunch menus. Voilà! There are your family's requirements for a year's food storage. Use this list as a shopping planner (watch for sales) and an inventory checklist. Also note that you don't need to have ambitions for a year's storage. You could start with a month's storage, or three, and tailor the math to your needs.

Finally, don't forget nonfood items like soap, shampoo, toilet paper, pet supplies, and so on.

2. Use It or Lose It

No food has an infinite shelf life. In fact, most foods begin to lose nutrition and palatability almost immediately. Over time, some foods even become unsafe. County extension services in all parts of the country have compiled lists of recommended storage durations for foods stored at room temperature, refrigerator temperature, and freezer temperature. Flour, for example, is only recommended for six to eight month's storage at room temperature. Many unopened foods last several months, but even the longest-storing foods are recommended for only about two years.

If food only lasts several months in prime condition, then it is clear that we must rotate food supplies to avoid throwing them away. And tossing food that is spoiled before you eat it is no different than tossing food that no one ate. If you follow the "store what you eat" approach, then rotating food is easy because you can use it up in your everyday cooking.

Rotation doesn't happen automatically. You must make it happen: date the foods as you buy/store them (use a crayon, wax pencil, or magic marker—put month and year on the label); put newer foods behind the older; and consciously use the older foods.

3. Store It Cool

Temperature, more than almost any other factor, determines the storage life of your food as well as its condition. For prepared foods and leftovers, for example, getting them into the refrigerator immediately can be a matter of safety.

Cooler storage temperatures slow the deterioration of food and the loss of nutrition and taste. Cooler is always better. Build shelves in the basement or a part of the house where the temperature is cool year-round. If you have the space and budget, consider buying an upright freezer for your storage area.

4. Be Safe

If there is any question about the safety of the food you have stored—in smell, taste, texture, appearance—throw it out. If a can is bulging, is leaking, or spurts when you open it, throw it out.

When canning, handle food in a clean area with clean hands. Don't change canning recipes or take shortcuts on processing. Recipes are carefully formulated and tested to assure your food will be safe. If you change anything, the acidity may be altered or the processing time and temperature may no longer be valid. Use only calibrated pressure canners (county extension services test pressure canners) for foods that require pressure processing.

For storage, remember that cooler is always better.

- **Refrigerator**: Keep it at 34–40°F

- **Freezer**: Keep it below 0°F, colder is better.

- **Always**: If you have any question about the safety of the food, throw it out.

• • •

Many of the ideas in this chapter are taken from county extension service pamphlets. The extension service is an excellent source of reliable information about food production and storage. Check online, or printed information can be purchased for about the cost of reproduction, and knowledgeable staff are ready to answer your questions.

Emergency preparedness
Do one thing today.

PREPAREDNESS SKILLS YOU OUGHT TO HAVE

Part 1 of this book has compiled a series of basic skills and principles that will serve you well in every emergency from the smallest daily crises to the largest area disasters. Knowledge and skills are the most valuable and versatile commodities you can store. They are infinitely updatable and never out of style. Furthermore, you always have them with you. To underscore these valuable skills, let's review.

Staying Calm

If you panic, you lose access to all of the other information in your head. Cultivate calm by planning, by being aware of the situation, and by practice, practice, practice.

- Create a family plan. A plan gives you focus in the first unsettled minutes of an emergency and changes your attitude from "victim" to "survivor."

- Situational awareness—paying attention to what's going on and what you might do if there is an emergency—cultivates calmness by reducing the surprise factor. Play the "what if?" mental game. What if there is an earthquake while I'm at the mall? What if there is a power outage tonight? What if the water is unsafe? Review and refresh your plan of action. If you don't know an answer, find out: read a book, ask a friend, or go online.

- Calmness can be practiced. Notice how you react to life's unexpected situations. The more you are aware of your reactions, the earlier you can catch and modify them. Then practice maintaining a cool exterior; a cooler interior will result.

Knowing CPR/First Aid

These skills are best learned from experts, and they need to be kept current. Techniques and tools are always improving, so if you learned these skills long ago, go back and refresh. The best source of training is an organization like the Red Cross, a local fire department, or a hospital. Expect to pay a modest fee for each of these classes and to commit several evenings to the training. Then build first-aid kits containing materials you are prepared to use. Assemble kits for home, car, and your pocket, if you spend time outdoors. Each will contain different items depending on the type of injuries that you might encounter.

Turning Off Utilities

Teach everyone in your family how and when to turn off the utilities. This includes knowing where the main shutoffs are and how to activate them. Include electricity, water, and gas.

Purifying Water

In many emergencies, there will still be water, but it may not be safe to drink. Learn to purify water by boiling, chemical treatment, and filtration. The most reliable sources of information include county and state health departments, FEMA (ready.gov), and the Centers for Disease Control and Prevention.

Cooking without a Stove

Even minor emergencies can leave you without conveniences. Learn to create healthy and tasty meals without your oven and range. Practice with the barbecue or a Dutch oven. Go camping and practice over an open fire—a tough skill to master. Camp gear makes a great emergency kitchen. Collect recipes and store emergency food supplies geared to non-stove cooking methods.

Finding Shelter and Warmth

Where would you stay if your house was uninhabitable in bad weather? Learn how and where to evacuate, and keep a grab-and-go kit available in case you don't get much warning. Camp trailers and tents are good emergency shelters. Learn to find or make shelter in the outdoors from survival handbooks, such as the *Boy Scout Fieldbook*.

Sanitation Skills

Teach good hygiene to all family members. Learn how to wash hands with limited water. Practice good food preparation techniques. Store trash bags to manage food wastes and keep pests at bay. Learn about expedient containment (and disposal) of human wastes if the toilets stop working for some time. Check with the county or state health department.

Cooperating

In an emergency, we all need each other, but that is when our nerves will be most frayed. Learn to work and play well with others. Emergencies are inconvenient for everyone, so practice patience. Meet your neighbors now, under less stress. Store "comfort" items, like teddy bears or toys for small children and entertainment items or treats for older children and adults. Pack earplugs in your evacuation kit to ease sleeping in a crowded shelter: everyone is more cheery with more sleep.

Improvising, Adapting

Nothing will go exactly as planned, so learn to adapt. Pack duct tape and baling wire. Pack multiple solutions for light, heat, cooking, and repairs. The skill of improvising can be cultivated. Practice while camping; resist the urge to go buy every little thing you forget. You can also practice having emergencies. Try living on your 72-hour kit, even for a day: turn off the power, avoid using the stove, ration water. See how creative you become.

Making Your Own Fun

What would life be without electronic entertainment? Maybe pretty fun. Learn to play simple games with few pieces or parts. Collect instructions for card games and parlor games. Store playing cards, dice, pencils and paper, and other items that support a variety of different games. Every now and then get out your emergency lights, make snacks from your emergency supplies, and play an old-fashioned board game.

Emergency preparedness:
Learn one skill today.

PREPAREDNESS FOR PEOPLE WITH STRENGTH, MOBILITY, OR DISABILITY CONCERNS

Disasters are especially hard on the elderly and people with disabilities. People with special medical or physical conditions should prepare for emergencies; who knows your abilities limitations better than you? As you plan, consider these adaptations to your situation:

Preparedness Plan

In addition to all of the plan elements in chapter 2, people with special needs also need to have a get-the-word-out plan. A person with these needs has already learned one of the key principles of preparedness: create a network and work together. If you have special needs, start your planning with a written list of all of the people in your life who help you meet your specific needs. This can include your medical team: doctors, pharmacists, therapists, in-home care, personal assistant, and so on. It may also include family members, neighbors, church members, care or agency personnel, and coworkers. You might also list your landlord and the handyman crowd: your plumber, fix-it guy, car mechanic, and yard-care service worker. From this network, identify those who are closest and most able to check in with you in case of an emergency and arrange for them to do so. Designate several checkers, in case conditions make it hard for the primary contact to get there. You may be able to register with a local hospital or the fire or police department to assure you are near the top of their lists as well. In addition to people checking on you, you also need to have a way to tell others when you are in distress. A debris-scattering earthquake that might be minor for others can be a big deal for someone in a wheelchair. Keeping a fully charged cell phone on you at all times is a must, and you might consider other options like medical alert systems, pagers, or a good old-fashioned whistle.

All of the elements of a reunion plan and a communications plan, including an out-of-state contact, still apply here, but your "get ready" plan may take some additional effort. For example, you may wish to train members of your network how to operate critical medical equipment, how to change batteries, and how to do basic maintenance. Keep copies of operating manuals close at hand. You may wish to put spare parts for your critical equipment in your emergency kit. If your equipment depends on electricity, contact the provider to find out about emergency backup power and other options for when the power goes out. If you use a powered scooter, you should have a manual wheelchair on hand for emergencies.

72–Hour Kit

The same principles and the same categories of supplies listed in chapter 3 still apply if you have special needs, but consider:

- Store food and water in packages that you can open with your strength and dexterity. If you use adaptive devices, consider getting extras to put with your kit. Store no-cook foods to reduce the obstacles to keeping up your energy and morale. Store smaller containers of water that are easier to lift, and make sure you have tools to help you get them open if your grip strength is low. Store your kit in a rolling container so you don't have to lift to move it, and make sure it is in an accessible place.

- If you are vision or hearing impaired, you will also need to consider how you will obtain critical information in an emergency, whether by an assistive device or by having someone help you. If you are hearing impaired, you may still want a battery-powered radio so an aide can listen and help you get the information.

- Include items for personal hygiene needs.

- Your first-aid kit should have extra supplies for dealing with the urgencies and emergencies that are unique to you own situation.

- Make sure you have extra medications on hand at all times. Check with your doctor about getting a prescription for a few days or weeks of extra medications. Keep a complete and up-to-date list of all medications you take, including the dosage and frequency.

Evacuation

Your home is your best refuge and the location of all of your resources, but there are times when you must leave it, sometimes immediately. Make sure you have two planned exits from each room and an outside meeting place to get back with your family or members of your team. If you have special medical needs, you may be able to prearrange with a hospital or other care facility for you to stay with them in case of a local or smaller-scale evacuation. Identify family or friends that might host you in case you need to get farther away. If you go to a public shelter, be sure your supplies and equipment are marked with your name to avoid confusion and loss in a busy place.

• • •

While it might seem that your special needs cause you to be vulnerable in an emergency, there are some silver linings: you already know that you need a network of people, you know who they are, and you know how to articulate your needs. You have experience being resourceful and determined, and overcoming obstacles. And if you do some planning and a little preparing, you can measurably boost your odds of getting safely through an emergency.

Emergency preparedness:
Do one thing today.

PART 2

RESPONDING TO EMERGENCIES

THE POTENTIAL
EMERGENCIES
AROUND US

Early in your family's preparation planning, you should assess which disasters are most likely in your area and your life and then focus your planning on those likely events. It would not be the best use of your time to prepare for a tsunami, for example, if you don't live on the coast. Even among those emergencies that are possible in your area, some are definitely more probable than others, so your first efforts should focus on the most probable risks. Also, you'll find that as you prepare for the likely events, you'll be more prepared for the less likely events, since many preparation principles are the same.

The following table lists some potential emergencies that you can sort though to determine your most likely risks. The first two columns list the emergencies and summarize who might be at an increased risk. This is just a starting point; you and your family should review each of the emergencies yourselves and decide on your level of risk.

In addition to listing the potential risks, the table shows the most likely scale of each risk. This information might be best used to determine how much help you might have and how extensively you must prepare to be on your own. For example, in a household accident, you can and should call immediately for public services like paramedics and ambulances. In a serious earthquake, however, public services may be so overtaxed that you will need to fend for yourself for some time.

First, read through the list of potential disasters and mark the ones that seem possible for your family or in your area. You may need additional research to uncover other risks that are specific to your area, like potential hazardous materials storage areas and transport routes. Don't forget to include a risk assessment for other locations where you spend time: work, school, shopping centers, and so on. If your list of possible emergencies is long, pick a couple to get started: I recommend house fires and power outages.

I have explicitly addressed many of these emergencies here in part 2. Because this book is intended as a basic guide and since some of the potential disasters are rare or require advanced preparation, some of them are not specifically treated in this book, but if you prepare for the most likely events, you'll be in pretty good shape for everything else.

The task of risk assessment and prioritization is easy to do, but don't let the magnitude of the preparation tasks discourage you. Remember some of the basic principles in this book: any preparation is better than no preparation; it doesn't have to be perfect; the best preparedness commodity to store is knowledge; and do a little bit every day. In fact, the most potent advice is to remember the theme of this book:

Emergency preparedness:
Do one thing today.

Disaster Risk Assessment

Disaster	Who is at Risk?	What's the Scale?				
		Personal	Neighborhood	City	Region	Nation
Accident, medical emergency	Everyone	×				
Avalanche	If you live in or travel through mountainous areas	×	×			
Cold, extreme	The entire US, but especially those areas where winter storms would be unexpected. Ice storms pose special risks				×	
Dam failure	If you live near a waterway with any man-made water storage. Includes dams, ponds, and large tanks		×			
Drought	Everyone					×
Earthquake	Almost all US. Especially California, Alaska, Mountain States, New Madrid fault zone, and upper New England				×	
Epidemic	Everyone			×	×	×
Financial panic	Everyone					×
Fire, house	Everyone	×				
Fire, wildfire	If your home is near wild lands or heavily wooded areas		×			
Floods, flash	If you live in drainage, like a canyon, narrow valley, or river bed		×			
Floods, river	If you live in a river floodplain		×	×		
Hazardous materials spill	Everyone, especially within a mile of highways, railways, waterways, pipelines, or storage depots		×			
Heat, extreme	Everyone				×	
Hurricane	If you live near ocean, especially Gulf Coast and Atlantic coast				×	

Disaster	Who is at Risk?	What's the Scale?				
		Personal	Neigh-borhood	City	Region	Nation
Landslide/ mudslide	If you live near steep slopes; could be developed or not		×			
Radiological accident	If you live within 25 miles of nuclear power plant, nuclear military facility, or spent fuel storage				×	×
Riot	If you live in urban area or attend large events, games, concerts, and so on			×	×	
Storm surge	If you live near the Gulf of Mexico or Atlantic Ocean				×	×
Stranded car	If you live or travel in remote areas or severe weather	×				
Terrorism	Everyone; low chance of being in an incident; high chance of being impacted by the reactions			×		
Tornado	Everyone; highest risk in central plains and southern states			×	×	
Tsunami	Any coastal area, especially West Coast					×
Unemployment	Everyone	×				
Utility failure	Everyone. Includes power, gas, water, and sewer	×		×	×	
Volcano	If you live near active volcano			×		
Volcano ashfall	If you live downwind of a volcano				×	
Winds, high	Everyone			×		

CASE STUDIES

9/11 Terrorist Attack

Summary

On September 11, 2001, a group of terrorists hijacked four airplanes. Two were intentionally flown into the towers of the World Trade Center in Lower Manhattan, one was flown into the Pentagon, and one crashed into a field in Pennsylvania after passengers fought to regain control. Because of the damage inflicted by the intense jet fuel fires, both towers collapsed, destroying or damaging a number of nearby structures. In addition to death, injuries, and destruction, there were nationwide interruptions to communications and transportation systems.

Results/Effects

- **Casualties:** 2,996 people died; over 6,000 were injured. An estimated 18,000 additional people developed health effects from dust and hazardous materials dispersed by the collapsing towers.

- **Economic effects:** The towers were destroyed, and a number of nearby buildings were severely damaged, many of which required demolition. The stock market tumbled when it reopened several days later; the stocks lost 1.4 trillion dollars over the next week. The New York economy lost about 2.8 billion dollars in work/wages over the next several months, and thousands of small businesses were destroyed.

- **Communications/transportation**: All commercial flights were immediately grounded, which lasted three days. Flights already airborne were diverted to the closest airports. The transportation upset stranded tens of thousands of people in unexpected locations. Communications equipment mounted on the North Tower and lines that routed through the World Trade Center were destroyed. Because of the highly localized nature of the attacks, communications were quickly rerouted through other hubs. Most of Manhattan's and Brooklyn's transportation—roads, ferries, subways, buses—was snarled for days.

- **Other**: Some looting was reported.

Preparedness Lessons Learned

1. The North Tower was struck first, and the damage destroyed stairwells so that no one above the point of impact had any escape route. Some tried to go to the roof, but access doors were locked, no rescue plan was in place, and the raging inferno made helicopter operations impossible. Many people in the South Tower evacuated when they saw the North Tower attacked, which saved thousands of lives. The South Tower impact left one staircase intact, allowing several dozen people above the point of impact to escape. It was reported that some dispatchers instructed people not to evacuate on their own but to wait for responders.

   Lessons: Usually it is best to follow the instructions of authorities, but in this case, those who correctly assessed the situation and made their own decision to evacuate early saved their lives. In an emergency, it is best to err on the side of conservatism. Whether you work in a high-rise or just visit occasionally, be sure you know multiple evacuation routes. This goes for hotels as well as office buildings.

2. There were alarms and warnings to evacuate the building. Although tower collapse was not immediately predicted, survival depended upon getting out of the buildings and away from the complex. It is estimated that over seventeen thousand people were in the World Trade Center complex when the attack began. The ones who survived are the ones who heeded the alarms and the warnings and got out of the building.

Lessons: Get out when told to get out. Don't delay, don't seek a second opinion, don't justify staying longer. Maybe even get out before being told.

3. The attacks on a few blocks comprising the WTC affected the whole Lower Manhattan area and hundreds of thousands of inhabitants, workers, and commuters. Tunnels and bridges were closed due to fears of subsequent attacks. The subway system was stopped. Bus routes were interrupted. Evacuation generally proceeded on foot, as taxis and cars were unable to access the larger affected area.

    Lessons: Prepare for a walking evacuation. People who had to walk long distances quickly found out if their shoes were good for walking. The attacks occurred on the morning of a mild autumn day; if they had occurred at night or on a winter's day, flashlights and/or coats would have been in demand. It is important to have an evacuation kit and plan. Because of the chaos, there were many families that had to wait for hours to find out if their loved ones were safe; a contact plan is an important part of your family plan. It may also be helpful to identify some nearby safe places to evacuate to that don't require you to walk for miles from work.

4. Travelers were stranded in all kinds of unexpected places. Planes already in the air were diverted to the nearest airport and grounded for days, heedless of inconvenience. Flights not yet started were cancelled. Rental cars quickly became scarce, even in cities hundreds of miles away from the disaster.

    Lessons: When traveling, keep a small emergency kit with some extra personal medications and supplies to tide you over during small delays and inconveniences. Some extra emergency cash could be helpful. Travel with a full water bottle (bring empty through security and refill at the gate) and a couple of energy bars.

Conclusion

Terrorism attempts to affect many people by a public attack on a smaller number. Our systems are still vulnerable to terrorism in ways we have not yet imagined: transportation, communications, food supply, medicine, water; and because of our media saturation, we are vulnerable to panic-inducing images and reports. The odds of being directly involved in such an attack are very low, but the consequences can affect anyone, nationwide or even worldwide. Because attacks can take a variety of forms, it is not possible to prepare for each permutation. But the core principles of preparedness—a communications plan, an evacuation plan, and a few emergency supplies at your place of work, in your luggage, or in your car—will give you options to respond if anything happens. And your ability to keep your cool and stay aware of the situation will enable you to reach out and pull someone along with you. The stories of survivors from 9/11 are full of gratitude and awe at the way people helped each other, in many cases saving lives.

Hurricane Katrina

Summary

On Monday, August 29, 2005, at about 6:00 AM, a Category 3 hurricane in the Gulf of Mexico with winds of about 125 miles per hour crossed the Louisiana coastline and headed toward New Orleans. A large storm surge breached the aging levee system and seawater flooded over 80 percent of the city. Damage was extreme, and casualties were worsened by a late and incomplete evacuation. The region was in chaos for days, with no utilities, little effective police presence, and lack of transportation and supplies.

Results/Effects

- **Casualties**: At least 1,833 people died in the hurricane and subsequent floods and chaos.

- **Economic effects**: Total property damage was estimated at 108 billion dollars.

- **Communications/transportation**: The majority of the roads into and out of the city were damaged, and the I-10 Twin Span Bridge collapsed. The airport closed and did not resume commercial flights for over a month. Cellular phone networks were destroyed, three million people in various states were left without power, and communications were completely disrupted in some areas, with HAM radio operators the only means of communications for days. A single AM radio station remained on the air for the first several weeks.

- **Other:** Reports of crime, looting, and violence were widespread, and the governor mobilized National Guardsmen to assist local law enforcement to restore order, which reportedly took about a week.

Preparedness Lessons Learned

1. The storm was tracked by the National Hurricane Center starting on August 23, nearly six days before it hit New Orleans. The possible impact on New Orleans was forecast as early as August 26, with watches turning to warnings as the day went on. By Sunday August 28, it was clear that it was a large storm and that New Orleans and all of the areas lower than sea level were vulnerable to the huge storm surge. Evacuation orders, both voluntary and mandatory, began to be issued as early as August 27. A mandatory evacuation order for New Orleans was issued about twenty hours before Katrina made land, but by then, it was too late for many. A large segment of the local population depended on public transit, which was idled by a lack of bus drivers. Although some 80 percent of the population evacuated, over a quarter million people were unable or unwilling to leave.

   Lessons: Get out when you are told to get out. Katrina's size and pathway were well known with sufficient time to evacuate, but officials started with "voluntary" evacuation orders, which were widely ignored. Maybe even get out before you are told to get out. Be aware of neighbors or friends that may not have resources or pathways to evacuate and assist them, as you are able.

2. The Louisiana Superdome was designated a "refuge of last resort" by the city, and preparations were made to feed fifteen thousand refugees; nearly thirty thousand showed up. About twenty-five thousand sheltered at the Civic Center, which had no preparations. In both locations, supplies were insufficient for the demand, sanitary conditions deteriorated rapidly, and relief did not arrive for days. Refugees were told there would be no supplies and to bring their own. There were few cots, no sick bay, and no medical responders on site. Reports of crime and violence were not officially confirmed, but safety was a continual concern.

   Lessons: The government cannot save you. Not the city, county, state, or federal governments. You must take responsibility for your own safety and your own response. Your preparations should include evacuation plans and contingencies so you can avoid the public shelters that may not be as well supplied or tightly controlled as you hope. Your 72-hour kit should be portable so you can take it with you, because there may not be other supplies for you. If you must go to a shelter or "refuge of last resort," you may need to take measures to improve your security by banding together with other trustworthy refugees, staggering your sleeping schedules, and keeping your own watch over those for whom you are responsible. And when your gut tells you that it is time to get out, get out.

3. The city of New Orleans has vast tracts of land that are below sea level. There are levees and dikes to protect the city, but it was apparently known before Katrina that a large storm surge could overtop and destroy the levees.

Lessons: While it is impossible to find a location that does not have some kind of natural hazard associated with it, most of the information you need to make a decision on where to buy or build a house is readily available. For example, FEMA manages a program to continually update floodplain mapping, and a quick reference to the proper map (at msc.fema.gov) will tell you your flood risk, and, as important, whether you'll be able to obtain flood insurance. There are similar maps for faults and earthquake risks, landslide risks, and even wildfire risks. It just makes sense to check things out.

4. After Superstorm Sandy pushed another unprecedented storm surge ashore in New York and New Jersey, residents of New Orleans sent messages to victims summarizing things they had learned. A large number of the messages advocated patience and persistence in rebuilding and extolled the benefits of doing it together as a community. They talked of personal and community strength born of facing adversity with their neighbors.

Lessons: In an emergency, your neighbors are going through the same things, and maybe worse. Knowing that the government is likely to be unable to help enough people, how will those with special needs get through it? By the care and concern of neighbors. Get to know your neighborhood and your neighbors before an emergency makes it necessary. Hold a summer barbecue, give them holiday wishes on special days, learn names, and understand special needs. Agree to check on each other in extreme circumstances, and when the need comes, you'll be better prepared to help others through it.

Conclusion

Wherever you live, there are hazards both natural and man-made. You can spend a little time learning of the hazards particular to your area. By knowing more about the vulnerabilities, you will better know what to do when extreme conditions are predicted. If you knew that you lived below sea level and the National Hurricane Center predicted a direct hit of a record storm, you would be able to decide how serious to consider the warning and how early to evacuate. Yes, your house might get flooded, but your staying wouldn't prevent that anyway. This kind of knowledge and preparation might spare you the experience of going to a public shelter and hoping someone will be able to take care of you. But if you've read this far, it is unlikely that you would expect someone else to take care of you anyway.

Tohoku Earthquake and Tsunami

Summary

On March 11, 2011, a magnitude 9.0 earthquake lasting six minutes struck off the coast of Tohoku, Japan. It was one of the five largest earthquakes recorded in the world since record keeping began and the most powerful to ever hit Japan. The earthquake triggered a 133-foot-high tsunami, which traveled inland up to six miles in some places. The tsunami was much more deadly and damaging than the earthquake itself. The earthquake and tsunami also led to cooling system failures at three nuclear reactors near the coast, which, in turn, led to fuel rod meltdowns, hydrogen gas explosions, and radiation leaks. Residents in a twelve-mile radius were evacuated; a fifty-mile radius was recommended.

Results/Effects

- **Casualties:** 15,881 people died, with 6,142 injured and 2,668 missing.

- **Economic effects**: 129,225 buildings were totally collapsed, with another nearly one million buildings sustaining damage. The earthquake resulted in about 30 billion dollars in insurance claims, while the World Bank estimated total economic impact at 235 billion dollars. The Tohoku earthquake/tsunami was therefore the most expensive natural disaster ever.

- **Communications/transportation**: Roads and railways were severely damaged by both the earthquake and the tsunami flooding. Airports, railways, and roads were all closed for some period. One and a half million households in northeastern Japan were left without water. And 4.4 million households were left without electricity.

- **Other**: The earthquake triggered at least one dam collapse, some liquefaction, and many fires.

Preparedness Lessons Learned

1. An analysis of the fatalities recovered in the first month revealed that about 93 percent of victims died by drowning. The non-drowning victims either died from internal injuries, were crushed, or died from burns. Only 58 percent of people in possibly dangerous coastal areas listened to tsunami warnings after the earthquake and headed for higher ground—only 5 percent of these people were caught in the tsunami. Almost half of the people who didn't heed warnings were hit. (Note that there was a warning system that gave Tokyo about a minute of warning before the ground waves reached the city, giving them time to duck and cover.)

   Lessons: The tsunami was the most deadly element of the disaster, and warnings based on the earthquake were provided to encourage evacuation. Even though the reach of the tsunami was unprecedented, the vast majority of those who tried to evacuate were spared the danger of the water. Those who didn't evacuate were much less fortunate. This might feel like a familiar phrase by now, but get out when you are told to get out. Maybe even get out before you are told, if you can figure it out for yourself.

2. Over 65 percent of all victims were sixty years old or older; 24 percent were in their seventies. After a year, it was reported that 70 percent of missing victims were sixty or older. This may be due to the demographics of those who were at home when the disaster struck.

Lessons: While sixty and seventy years old is not particularly elderly, and while it is not clear that the elderly were victims because of their age or associated infirmities, in general the elderly and those with strength or mobility issues are more vulnerable in disasters. Those with strength or mobility concerns can prepare for emergencies and should plan to have additional family and neighbor connections to help them out in times of need. See chapter 9.

3. There was at least one derailed train in the region; passengers were not rescued until the next morning. Because it was early March, the nights were chilly.

Lessons: When traveling by any mode, keep a small emergency kit with some extra personal medications and supplies to tide you over during small inconveniences. Dress for travel with the idea that you may have to leave the vehicle in an emergency, and take seasonal and weather conditions into account. Some extra emergency cash could be helpful. Travel with a full water bottle and a couple of energy bars.

4. The earthquake and tsunami caused failure of some critical cooling systems at coastal nuclear facilities. There were explosions from hydrogen gas buildup, and radiation leaks resulted in the evacuation of surrounding communities to a radius of twelve miles, though fifty was recommended.

Lessons: There are power plants, factories, chemical processing plants, and all kinds of man-made risks all around us. You need to know about the risks in order to plan for them. The good news is that your community may have already catalogued these potential hazards and developed response plans for similar emergencies. Call your city hall and see if a local emergency planning council has been created and if a city emergency plan exists. The bad news is that it may not exist or may be badly outdated. If you know what the risks are and how close to them you are (there are a number of easy-to-use map applications on the Internet), you can plan evacuation routes and destinations and be ready to go when alerted.

5. Supplies of water, food, and medicine were delayed in the first week after the earthquake. Many shelters were undersupplied with food, water, and medical equipment, and poor sanitary conditions developed. Early spring temperatures and electrical and gas outages exacerbated difficulties.

Lessons: Even in civic-minded, authority-respecting Japan, the government was unable to care for all who needed it. Each family must develop evacuation and communication plans and prepare to be on its own for three to seven days.

Conclusion

The 2011 Tohoku earthquake/tsunami has many relevant lessons for us because it has so many different elements, each with its own character. This disaster was unique because of its intensity and size; it was completely unprecedented. Because of this, it is tempting to say, "There will always be an emergency bigger and badder than we expect, so we cannot plan for it." While it is true that there will always be record-setting disasters, it does not follow that planning and preparing are futile. The nature and idiosyncrasies of any disaster will undoubtedly disrupt the smooth flow of your plans, but having them as a starting point and having the attitude that you must take care of yourself puts you in a stronger position to weather the crisis. And any preparation is better than no preparation.

Superstorm Sandy

Summary

On October 29, 2012, Sandy—a post-tropical cyclone with a circulation spanning over one thousand miles—pushed a record storm surge ashore in New Jersey and New York, flooding tunnels and subways and coastline communities. Sandy was called a superstorm, not only because of its size but also due to the influence of two other storm systems—one that deflected it back to the west toward land and one that brought additional moisture and colder temperatures. Accurate strength and trajectory predictions from the National Hurricane Center enabled states to issue evacuation orders and to implement other measures such as school and business closures to reduce the impact and hasten the recovery. Coastal flooding damaged many shore properties. The high winds and the extensive coastal flooding knocked out power to over 5 million people in the New York/New Jersey area alone; power outage and transportation restart were inconveniences to many millions of people in the area for days and sometimes weeks.

Results/Effects

- **Casualties**: An estimated 285 people died in multiple countries, from the Caribbean to Canada.

- **Economic effects**: The economic impact was variously estimated at between sixty and eighty billion dollars in damage in just the United States.

- **Communications/transportation**: Thousands of flights were cancelled, and subway, rail, and bus services were suspended as Sandy approached. Subway tunnels were flooded, and bridges and roads were either damaged or covered by debris. The restart of public transit took days, and it was weeks before it ran smoothly again for the millions who depend on it. Power outages made fuel dispensing difficult, and damaged pipelines or closed roads and bridges made resupply impossible for days, necessitating rationing.

- **Other**: Coastal flooding did the most visible damage and was reported widely in the press. Inland, downed trees were responsible for extended power outages. Where flooding occurred, the water was often polluted with raw sewage after pumps lost power. In other cases, hazardous chemicals and wastes were washed into flood waters, creating further hazard.

Preparedness Lessons Learned

1. An analysis of over one hundred fatalities in the northeast United States reveals some patterns: over a third died from drowning, either in their homes or in their cars. The second highest cause of death was falling trees, and the third highest cause of death was slips and falls, particularly among the elderly. In fact, about half of the victims were people over age sixty-five. A cause of death in a significant number of victims was carbon monoxide poisoning from portable generator fumes.

    Lessons: The landfall of Sandy was accurately predicted days prior to its actually happening. Every single person in Sandy's path had warning and time enough to evacuate. Just as in 9/11, Katrina, or Tohoku, the same lesson is repeated here: if you want to save your life, get out when you are told to get out. Maybe get out *before* you are told to get out. If your home is going to be flooded by the storm surge, you can do nothing by being there, and your presence means nothing but danger to you and perhaps to the brave responders who may be called out to rescue you.

In any emergency, the elderly are disproportionately affected, whether by health or mobility issues, or by location, or by lack of resources. If you aren't as spry as you used to be, or if you have health or mobility issues, you need to develop a network of people you can call on for help. It may be family if you are fortunate enough to have some in the area; it may be kind neighbors who can look in on you; it may be social agencies that serve you; or it may be a church "family" that can help you out. Many people are happy to help and simply need to be alerted to your need.

Also, in emergencies, common sense often takes a holiday. People try to do things they would not ordinarily think of doing and get into situations where accidents can happen more readily. In Sandy, several people were injured by chain saws. There were electrocutions, car accidents, heart attacks, and the aforementioned falls and asphyxiations. The best thing to do in an emergency is stop, take a deep breath, and approach every task with sense and caution. All of the circumstances and urgencies of an emergency will quickly pass, even if you don't climb on your roof with a chain saw in the middle of a storm.

2. Falling trees took out thousands of power lines. Even though utility companies pre-positioned response crews and brought in outside help, many people were without power for days and weeks. Sandy highlighted the fact that our national power grid is fragile and vulnerable to just about any emergency.

Lessons: We depend upon electricity for so much, and we take our mobile phones, which didn't do much a decade ago, for granted. Our phones have become our lifelines to so many things we do, including work, family, and even social connections. We use them to get news and information about the weather. They store our reference information, our contact list, our address collection, maps, and even account numbers and passwords. But the batteries only last a day or two, and then they need to be recharged. A number of products on the market right now, with more emerging all the time, will recharge your phone by deep-cycle batteries, solar cells, or temporary generation. Make sure you have several backup plans for keeping this important tool alive in the most critical of times, and make sure you have several recharge cords available.

3. For the largest majority of those affected, Sandy boiled down to a long power outage and transportation/commuting difficulties. For a few days, fuel shortages led to rationing, long lines, and short tempers. With no power to traffic signals, each intersection became a four-way stop, except when it became a no-way stop. Stores were picked bare, and resupply was slow in reestablishing.

Lessons: Really, no one is prepared for a weeks-long power outage. Veterans of Sandy learned valuable lessons that can serve us:

- You need water storage. A case or two of bottled water doesn't go very far.

- You need fuel. If you have a fireplace to heat your home, you should try to calculate how much wood it takes to heat the house all day and into a cold night.

- The smallest things become big things. Patience is in short supply too.

- Cash is crucial. Without power, you can't use your credit card, no matter how much money is in the bank.

- Food storage is worthless if you can't or don't know how to prepare it or the kids won't eat it. And you need a lot more food when everyone is home all day.

- It is well and good to feed your own kids, but what will you do when the neighbor's kids come around? Sandy brought us many heartwarming stories of people helping each other through it all. It also brought us stories of frayed nerves, looting, and shootings.

- Plan some comfort items as well. After a few days, you'll need a cup of cocoa or a bite of chocolate. Have some board or card games to play and have a guitar around.

- When the trucks stopped rolling, the first things to become scarce during Sandy were fuel, matches/lighters, toilet paper (think about that one for a minute), paper plates and cups, milk, bread, aspirin and cold medicines, and anything to do with a portable generator.

Conclusion

Superstorm Sandy brought disaster home to the nation's most populous urban center. Millions of people were affected by power outages and shortages of food, fuel, and just about everything else. For a minority of people, the emergency was about high winds and storm surges that brought water and sand into their yards and houses. In many of those cases, the homeowners were uninsured for that kind of flooding. For millions more, it was simply dark and cold and really hard to get supplies for days. Can it happen to you? And will you be prepared to weather it? Heroic action isn't needed, just a survivor's attitude and the willingness to do one thing today.

• • •

Disasters and emergencies always present the same challenges to all of us: what you can get done before, especially if there is some warning; how you can best ride it out and stay alive; and how soon you can get back to normal after. In each of these large disasters and in countless smaller ones, there are similarities that can motivate us to do something today.

- What can you do before? Get some stuff together that will not be available in an emergency.
- What can you do during? Get out when you are told. Otherwise, keep your calm, use common sense, and stay alive.
- What can you do after? Be resourceful, be helpful to your neighbors, and be patient and optimistic: it will pass.

And do one thing today—every day.

HOUSE FIRES

A Too-Common Emergency

When we think of emergency preparedness, we often think of hurricanes, tornadoes, and earthquakes. But consider this: in 2011 in the United States, there were hundreds of thousands of house fires, killing over two thousand people and injuring almost fourteen thousand more, not counting firefighters. While major earthquakes are difficult to predict, and impossible to prevent, many of these too-common house fires can be prevented or mitigated. Here are some fire safety tips.

Prepare to Prevent Fires

- Practice safety in the kitchen; cooking equipment is the leading cause of all house fires. Clean up and remove combustible materials from around the stove. Don't let grease build up. Keep your attention on the stove; never leave it unattended. Especially don't leave children unattended in the cooking area. Don't use cloth dish towels as hot pot holders, especially if you have a gas stove with an open flame. Long sleeves with loose-fitting cuffs can be a fire hazard in the kitchen. Keep a fire extinguisher in plain sight.

- Most house fires occur from December through March. Space heaters can be dangerous. Keep them at least three feet from combustible materials like bedspreads, curtains, and clothing. Never drape wet clothes over them to dry. Never leave space heaters operating while sleeping. Never leave them unattended. Frequently check wires for fraying or overheating.

- Be smoker wary. Provide smokers with deep, stable ashtrays. Empty ashtrays daily; make sure that all butts are out cold. Make it an ironclad rule that no one smokes in bed.

- Treat electricity with respect. Buy only lab-tested (such as UL) electrical devices. Do not overload sockets or extension cords. Make sure all outlets have cover plates. If there are small children in your home, invest in socket covers too. Do not run wires under rugs, or puncture the cords with nails or staples. Replace worn wires on appliances and lights—this is easier and cheaper than replacing all of your belongings after a house fire. If you live in a house with a fuse box, be sure that the proper-sized fuses are installed. If a fuse keeps blowing, check the circuit for overload; don't just install a larger fuse.

- Teach fire safety to your children. Teach the smallest to tell an adult about any matches or lighters they find. Store matches and lighters out of children's reach.

- Clean up your storage and work areas. If you need an excuse to throw out piles of papers, magazines, and other junk, do it for fire safety. Throw out the old half-cans of paint and solvents. (Be sure to dispose of them properly. Many communities and waste management companies have annual hazardous waste collections for materials like these.) Store the flammable materials you need to keep in original, marked, metal containers out of reach of children and outside the house in a shed. Never store flammables near heat and flame sources like the furnace and water heater.

- Protect your house from fireplace sparks by putting up a metal or tempered glass screen. Have the flue checked regularly to see that it is in good working order and that creosote is not building up. Make sure that the chimney has a spark arrestor screen on the outlet. Don't burn paper in your fireplace.

- Strictly enforce fireworks safety rules. Adults should supervise all fireworks. Light only one item at a time and keep all spectators at a safe distance. Douse used fireworks in a bucket of water and keep a hose ready. Only use fireworks on clean, flat surfaces. Follow all directions and keep away from homes, trees, and dry grass or weeds. Never point or throw fireworks at others.

Prepare to Minimize Damage and Injury

- Install and maintain smoke detectors. Install one on each level of your home and near each sleeping area. Check detector function once a month and replace batteries every nine to twelve months. Have children help you check the smoke detectors so they will hear and recognize the warning signal. Replace smoke detectors over ten years old. Install carbon monoxide (or CO) detectors. They can alert you to a buildup of carbon monoxide, a poisonous gas created by incomplete combustion, caused by malfunctioning furnaces and other flame appliances.

- Sleep with your bedroom doors closed. This slows the spread of smoke and fire.

- Make plans to escape a burning house. Identify at least two exits from every room. Make sure everyone knows how to open windows. If you have second floor bedrooms, have a fire ladder in each bedroom. Designate a safe spot outside of your home where everyone will gather after evacuation. Practice emergency escaping and reassembling at the designated spot twice a year. Caution: If your small children must exit a second floor bedroom, you can practice all but the dangerous descent procedure.

- Train the children, even the smallest, when and how to use 911. Teach them what to say when they call in an emergency. Help them understand the seriousness of using 911.

- Keep multipurpose (ABC) fire extinguishers handy in several places in your home: kitchen, basement, shop, garage, and car. Learn how to use them. Learn when to fight a fire and when it would not be safe. Watch the dial to know when to recharge or replace them.

Prepare to React Safely If a Fire Strikes

- Get out and stay out. Call for help on a neighbor's phone. Meet the rest of your family at the gathering spot so you'll know when everyone is out. Reentering a burning building without proper training and equipment could result in you becoming another victim.

- If trapped in a burning building, stay low and crawl under smoke and heat. If trapped in an upper story with no escape route, hang a sheet out of a window so rescuers know you need assistance.

- Test doors with the back of your hand before opening. If they are hot, don't open the door; use your second exit.

- If your clothes catch on fire, stop, drop, and roll to smother the flames.

• • •

A house fire is more likely than many of the disasters we usually worry about. It is also more preventable than many other emergencies. Fire safety is often about good housekeeping, paying attention, and using common sense, but like all other emergency preparedness, it requires that you take time—with your family—to learn and implement these suggestions.

Emergency preparedness:
Do one thing today.

EARTHQUAKES

Find and Fix Hazards before a Quake Shakes Up Your Life

Almost all of the United States has some risk of earthquake, although risks are highest along the Pacific Coast, Alaska, the Mountain States, the New Madrid region of Missouri, and the upper New England region. For example, experts tell us there is about a one in seven chance of a magnitude 7.0 earthquake along Utah's populous Wasatch Front in the next fifty years. Experts also tell us, though we don't always listen to this part, that the chances of smaller quakes are much higher. Although a magnitude 5.5 quake is one hundred times smaller than a 7.5, it can still topple furniture, break glass, and rearrange your interior decorating. Find and fix home hazards now so your house will be a safer place in a quake, big or small.

Go through each room imagining what would happen if the house began to shake side-to-side. Did you know that over half of the injuries from an earthquake are caused by falling objects and not collapsing buildings? Make a list of things to fix as you go through each area. Pay special attention to places where you spend a lot of time sitting or sleeping.

- Rearrange furniture so pieces that could topple or "walk" won't block exits.

- Secure tall furniture, like bookshelves and china hutches, to wall studs with straps or earthquake safety hardware from the hardware store. Be sure the hardware attaches to studs and not just into the drywall.

- Install lips or restraining wires on shelves to keep items from vibrating off. Look into earthquake putty or museum wax to secure items on open shelves

- Move the heaviest objects to the lowest shelves.

- Put hanging light fixtures on closed hooks. It's best not to hang plants, but if you must, use plastic pots and make sure they can't swing into windows.

- Aquariums are top heavy; attach them securely to stable stands or attach to a wall.

- Televisions, computers, and other heavy items can slide off flat surfaces. Install restraining straps or mount with hook and loop (Velcro-type) fasteners. Note that sticky-backed fasteners can mar furniture when removed.

- Hang heavy pictures from sturdy, closed hooks or wrap the wire around the hanger.

- Make sure no heavy or glass items—mirrors, heavy frame pictures—can fall onto beds. Move beds away from windows. Insist that kids straighten up rooms—exit pathways must be kept clear.

- Sliding doors should be of tempered glass.

- There are extra hazards in the kitchen. Wedge refrigerator rollers so it won't move. Consider child latches on cabinets so dishes don't become missiles. Make sure gas appliances have flexible couplings.

- Cleaning supplies, yard chemicals, paints, solvents, and even medicines can become hazards if they fall and spill. The first storage priority is to keep chemicals out of children's reach, but, where possible, store heavy containers low in locked cabinets. Avoid glass containers. Build restraining bars across open shelving or secure containers to wall with wires or elastic cords.

- One of the most important things you can do is secure your water heater to a brace (check with your gas company for details; see pages 88–90) or a wall. Replace "hard" gas couplings with flexible connectors.

- Locate main utility shutoffs and make certain they are accessible now and won't be buried by your belongings in a quake.

- Outside, check your AC or evaporative cooler; it might need additional bracing. Brace a masonry chimney and determine where pieces might fall. If you don't have solid sheathing on your roof, you can protect occupants by making a protective apron around the chimney. Screw plywood to the ceiling joists in the attic.

- Now that you are hazard-conscious, repeat your hunt at work or school. Then take your list and begin to work through it. Do the easy things first but persevere until you finish the tough ones too.

Misconceptions about When "The Big One" Hits

What can you expect when "the big one" hits? Some people focus too closely on the first, confusing, media-saturated hours after a quake and end up drawing inaccurate conclusions that could result more in hysteria than useful preparation. Here are some misconceptions people may have about what life will be like after a large earthquake.

Misconception: Expect no support from your community after an earthquake.

There is some truth in this statement: one lesson of the Tohoku earthquake (Japan 2011) is that the government cannot be expected to meet every citizen's every need in an emergency. But on the other hand, our entire society will not collapse with the overpasses. First, not every area of an earthquake zone will be hit equally hard. The location of the earthquake, its magnitude, soil structure, type and age of construction, and other factors combine to determine the severity of damage in a specific location. Neighborhoods right next to each other can experience dramatically different results. Nearby communities will have the ability to help the more severely impacted, especially after the first hours when the situation becomes clear.

Yes, emergency crews will be overwhelmed after an earthquake. But not too many on-duty, off-duty, or volunteer responders will abandon their posts. Medical and emergency responders are professionals who have worked years to develop their skills; to suggest they will bolt from their stations at the first sign of trouble would be simply unfair.

They are guided not only by their employers but also by their ethics and integrity. In other quakes, emergency personnel have performed heroically.

Misconception: There will be no utilities or services for weeks. Stores will be picked clean.

Water, sewer, electricity, gas, and phone services are all likely to be interrupted, and maybe over a wide area. Go ahead and kiss them good-bye, but don't be teary—they'll be back. They'll be back in hours for many, days for most others, and weeks only in isolated instances. Stores are more likely to be closed immediately following a quake than to be picked clean. Aisles will be clogged with fallen merchandise; electric registers won't work without power; and store employees that remain will have a huge mess to clean up before they can serve customers. After they open, resupply will be determined by the condition of the roads, and it may take some days to reestablish supplies to each store. This probably means that you'll have to range a little farther for a while. Fuel rationing is possible, but if necessary will only last a few days. In Superstorm Sandy (2012), rationing lasted about two weeks, mostly due to inability of tanker trucks to get to individual stations. Pumps will likely shut down from lack of electricity but will work again when power is restored.

Misconception: Rampaging fires will destroy everything.

We can expect some fires. Gas lines may be ruptured by ground movement and ignited by electrical sparks in isolated incidents. Other earthquakes have shown that unsecured water heaters tip over and rupture gas lines, which can then be ignited in a number of ways. In the Tohoku earthquake, wooden and paper structures collapsed onto cooking fires and stoves and some neighborhoods were burned. Lack of water will complicate firefighting. Fire risk will be highest where buildings are close together. In the suburbs, well-spaced houses and open expanses should mean that the inevitable fires will be mostly isolated and contained.

Misconception: All buildings will collapse. All roads will be impassable.

In recent earthquakes in Turkey, Haiti, and Iran, large temblors destroyed wide swaths of unreinforced masonry buildings. But in the United States, unless you live in an unreinforced masonry home (wood frame with brick facade doesn't count), it is likely that your house will remain habitable even if damaged. Single-family, wood-frame homes built in compliance with building codes can be expected to sustain little structural damage. This is especially true of one- or two-story structures on soft soils like clay, where earthquake waves are larger but farther apart. Higher frequency waves that might damage smaller buildings may occur in rocky areas. Although cracks may appear in roads and slabs, stretches of most roads will likely be passable or easily cleared, and any ground rupture will be limited and close to the fault. Long-span and older overpasses are at risk, but the freeway reconstruction constantly upgrades bridges and spans to more stringent earthquake standards, which will increase the probability of continued passability.

Misconception: Injuries will be untreated; bodies will lie unrecovered in the rubble; disease will be rampant.

A large earthquake will cause injuries, perhaps even fatalities. But life-threatening injuries will still receive care by medical professionals, although conditions may not be optimal. The injured may have to be transported to hospitals by friends, and medical facilities may sustain their own damages, but health-care professionals will still provide the best possible services. Minor injuries will probably have to wait longer for care, but that is expected in a large-scale disaster. Recovery of bodies will be swift. Disposal of human waste could be a problem, and unsanitary conditions could contribute to spread of disease. But most people do not stay long at shelters; if there are outbreaks, they will likely stay localized.

Misconception: There is nothing you can do.

Each earthquake has its own character, its own surprises. Things could be locally much worse or much better than described here. But don't panic; effective preparation requires calm thinking and deliberate action. First, although "the big one" is possible, smaller quakes are certain. Realize that even a modest quake can displace your belongings and disrupt your life. True, you cannot prevent or even predict earthquakes, but you do have some control over how much it affects you. Gather your family and make some plans. Identify the safest spots in each room to "duck, cover, and hold." Secure furniture that might fall; move heavy items from top shelves or above beds. Strap down your water heater and connect the gas with a flexible coupling. Secure hazardous materials to avoid spills. Designate an out-of-state friend for everyone in the family to contact; long distance may be easier than local calls, and you can leave messages. Gather some emergency supplies for a 72-hour disaster kit and take a first-aid course from the Red Cross or a comparable organization. Practice locating your utility shutoffs; practice stepping to your safe spots; practice having the lights off for a few hours one night. Talk with your neighbors about how to check on and help each other in a crisis. Do they have special needs? Where are their utility shutoffs?

Finally, many counties sponsor community emergency response team (CERT) training, and most communities have volunteer emergency preparedness committees. Invest some time and effort to assure that people get help from their communities, which include neighbors as well as governments. Things will be a mess for a while after an earthquake, but the situation is far from hopeless; your own preparedness will serve your family, and your communities and neighborhoods will come together to help each other.

How to Secure Your Water Heater

One of the most important things you can do to prepare for an earthquake is to secure your water heater. This action will prevent your water heater from toppling in an earthquake. Not only will you reduce the risk of broken gas lines and fire or explosion, but you will also preserve thirty to fifty gallons of drinking water.

Securing your water heater consists of two things: (1) immobilizing the water heater so it will not fall over, and (2) installing flexible couplings so any slight movements the water heater may make won't rupture the gas line.

Immobilize the Water Heater

There are many sound methods for preventing your water heater from toppling. Follow these guidelines for maximum safety:

- If you have a thirty- to fifty-gallon water heater within twelve inches of a stud wall, follow the directions on the diagram on page 90. This is not the only approach; another method, for example, uses L-shaped shelf braces to immobilize the water heater from each side.

- If your water heater is within twelve inches of a concrete wall, the same method will work, but you'll need to use ¼-inch expansion bolts to attach to the wall.

- If your water heater is more than twelve inches from a stud wall, there are commercial earthquake braces available. A licensed engineer or plumber will be able to recommend a sound method, or check with the gas company for recommendations.

- Make sure all of the connections to the wall attach to studs. Attachments to sheetrock alone will not be strong enough to hold a bucking water heater.

- Only nonflammable materials like metal straps and spacers should contact the water heater. Take special care to not create any fire hazards.

- If you have any questions, consult a licensed plumber or engineer.

Install Flexible Couplings

Although many newer houses already have flexible couplings on the water heater, many older houses have rigid gas connections. If you are not certain which type of connection you have, contact a plumber. If you have rigid connections, have a licensed plumber install a flexible, corrugated metal hose where the gas line connects to the water heater.

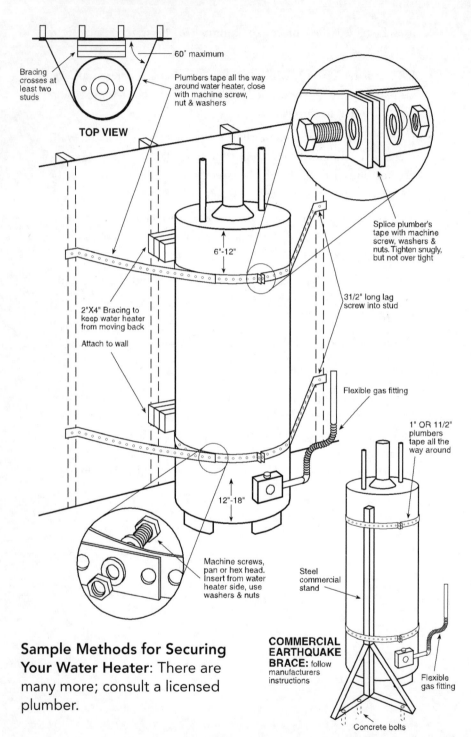

60° maximum

Bracing crosses at least two studs

Plumbers tape all the way around water heater, close with machine screw, nut & washers

TOP VIEW

Splice plumber's tape with machine screw, washers & nuts. Tighten snugly, but not over tight

6"-12"

2"X4" Bracing to keep water heater from moving back

Attach to wall

31/2" long lag screw into stud

Flexible gas fitting

1" OR 11/2" plumbers tape all the way around

12"-18"

Machine screws, pan or hex head. Insert from water heater side, use washers & nuts

Steel commercial stand

Flexible gas fitting

Sample Methods for Securing Your Water Heater: There are many more; consult a licensed plumber.

COMMERCIAL EARTHQUAKE BRACE: follow manufacturers instructions

Concrete bolts

What Do You Do after an Earthquake?

So, you've done a home hazard hunt and fixed things in your house that could be hazardous in a quake. You've secured your water heater so it won't topple, and you've installed flexible couplings so the gas line won't rupture. You've worked out a family emergency plan and put together a 72-hour kit so you have some ready resources in case of emergency. Just a few more quake-related items to discuss, and you'll be in pretty good shape.

Decide in advance where you want to ride out a quake. Identify a safe spot or two in every room. Remember that the ground motion will make it hard to move more than a step or two. Safe places include doorways, hallways, and wall corners where the building structure is strongest. Underneath sturdy tables and counters can be safe, although, in general, kitchens are full of hazards. Stay away from fireplaces (falling bricks, stones, or flues), windows and mirrors, bookcases, and tall furniture. Also try to stay aware of safe/hazardous spots in stores, malls, schools, and other public places. In a pinch, drop to the floor, scoot over to a wall, and cover your head.

When an earthquake hits, you'll have little warning, and it may take a second or two to realize what's happening, but there may be many more seconds of shaking ahead. In the Tohoku earthquake, shaking lasted for about six minutes. What should you do?

- Stay calm. Your best emergency tool is between your ears; don't lose it.

- Stay put. If inside, stay inside. If outside, stay outside. People are injured by falling debris at building entrances. The possible exception to this is in a downtown area with tall glass buildings. If there are no open spaces to get to, you may be better off getting in a nearby building. If you are in a car, stop as quickly as safety will allow. Pull off to the side if you can. Never stop on a bridge or under an overpass. Stay in the car until the quake is over. After, proceed cautiously, watching for road damage and debris.

- Take cover. If the stove is on, turn it off first. Move quickly to your safe place and stay alert. You may as well enjoy the ride; there's nothing you can do to stop it.

- As soon as the quake is over, make sure everyone is all right. Don't move any seriously injured people unless they are still in danger. Administer first aid. Get help.

- Minimize travel immediately after a quake. If you are not at home, reuniting with your family is a priority, but listen to the radio to determine if you can travel safely. If not, stay put. The situation will stabilize in a few hours; take enough care and time to get home safely.

- Put on sturdy shoes. Broken glass and tripping hazards may abound.

- Check for damage to electricity, water, and gas lines. Turn off the power and do not use matches or open flames until you are sure there is no fire hazard. Do not use the fireplace until you are certain the chimney is not damaged. Turn off your water where it enters your home. Even if your house pipes are fine, a broken main could siphon water from the pipes and water heater. There are many gallons of usable water in the pipes, and shutting the valve protects them.

- *Do not* turn off the gas immediately, unless you smell gas, see broken pipes, hear gas hissing, or are instructed to by authorities. If you do turn it off, you must call the gas company to check your appliances, restart your gas, and relight your pilot lights. It could take days for the gas company to get to you.

- Check for other hazards in your home. Sweep up glass, clean up spilled cleaners, chemicals, and medicines. Use caution.

- Comfort each other. Stay with children and reassure them.

- Check your home for structural damage. If uncertain, leave the home; you may have to wait for an engineer's inspection to be sure your home is safe.

- Check household sewer lines for damage before using the toilet.

- Call the out-of-town contact you identified in your family plan. Otherwise, stay off the phone unless you have a serious injury/ rescue situation.

- Check on your neighbors and others as you have arranged.

- Listen to your radio for updates and instructions.

- Do not go sightseeing.

- Be aware of the possibility of aftershocks.

- Don't forget to eat and drink something on a regular schedule. You'll feel much better. Remember to only use charcoal broilers outdoors.

- Practice good sanitation. Wash your hands frequently—this would not be a good time to get sick.

- In some cases, people are reluctant to go back into their homes to sleep. If this is the case, go to a nearby shelter or even camp out in your yard.

- Be patient and flexible.

- One final note: the first few hours after a quake may be confusing and stressful, but no matter how bad things seem to be, they will get better, and help will come.

Emergency preparedness:
Do one thing today.

HAZARDOUS MATERIALS

A Hazardous Materials Accident in Our Town?

On a cold day one December, a tank truck carrying propane rolled over on the main freeway. The next day, a truck carrying sodium azide (airbag propellant) overturned on a nearby road and caught fire, sending a potentially hazardous plume across the local area. The next day, on the emergency detour route, several containers of sulfur dioxide tumbled off a trailer, causing more concern.

Our modern society requires a lot of chemicals, some of them hazardous, to produce the lifestyle we enjoy. During production, storage, transportation, use, and disposal, these chemicals can be accidentally released, creating a potential for harm. Considering the vast quantities of chemicals produced and used, very few hazardous material ("hazmat") accidents actually occur. The Pipeline and Hazardous Materials Safety Administration (PHMSA) notes that while the amount of hazardous material transport has increased nearly 50 percent in the past twenty-five years, a person in the United States is three times as likely to be killed by lightning as by an accident involving hazardous materials during transportation.

Could a hazmat accident happen in your town? There are many potential sources of hazardous materials. Our communities encompass freeways, highways, waterways, and rail corridors. These arteries transport many things, including some hazardous materials. Local chemical plants and refineries produce chemicals. Local industries also store and use materials that can be hazardous. Farmers and ranchers use fertilizers and pesticides that can be hazardous in large quantities. The chlorine used to treat drinking water or sanitize swimming pool water can be a hazard if released in quantity. Even gasoline stations and the natural gas lines that serve our homes and churches could be sources of hazardous materials.

Our communities regularly have minor hazmat accidents that are handled quickly and efficiently by highly trained fire and hazmat crews. But occasionally, an incident escalates and grabs headlines for days. Recently in New Jersey, a highly used bridge over a waterway failed, dumping several tanks full of potentially hazardous chemicals into the water. Nearby residents were immediately evacuated, but as the difficulty of recovering the tankers became obvious, the evacuation radius became wider. Residents were out of their homes for days. Although most hazmat incidents are minor, there are several things we can do to be more prepared in case a major event does occur.

Before a Hazmat Accident

- Be aware of the hazards around you. Federal laws enable communities and interested citizens to learn about the types of materials stored and used in the community. This process starts with a phone call to local authorities who may have established a local emergency planning council ("LEPC" in government parlance) to identify and monitor hazardous materials. The laws are clear: communities and residents have a right to know what chemical hazards are in their midst.

- Support zoning decisions that group industrial activities together and adequately protect high population and residential areas from accidents. Support tough penalties for those who break the law in using or disposing hazardous materials: up to three hundred thousand hazardous waste sites dot the United States, many of them caused by illegal dumping.

- Prepare to evacuate at a moment's notice. Store your 72-hour kits in a container that you can grab on the way out—you may not have any time to pack anything else. Keep a list of other items you would like to take if you have time.

- Discuss with your family where you can go and who you should contact if you have to leave your neighborhood or if you are not allowed into it due to a hazmat incident. Establish an out-of-state contact that everyone in the family can call—collect, if necessary—to relay information between separated family members. (This is the same person you should call in an earthquake if local phone service is disrupted.) Keep this phone number in your wallet, purse, or backpack.

During a Hazmat Accident

In a hazmat accident, authorities may evacuate residents up to five miles downwind from the spill. Their first job is to protect human life. If you are directed to evacuate, gather your family and go. Grab your kit if it's handy, but do not stop to pack or prepare your house unless authorities allow it, which is unlikely. Make your way to your pre-arranged family contact point or a designated public shelter using an approved route. Do not take shortcuts or cross barriers; you could end up in a contaminated area. Report to your out-of-state contact.

If you are the first on the scene of a highway or rail accident that may involve hazardous material, remember: responding to hazmat incidents requires training (hundreds of hours of class and field work for experts) and specialized clothing, gear, and even breathing apparatus. If you don't have these things, do not approach the site, even if there may be injuries. There may be hazards that you cannot smell or see, and shifting winds can trap you in hazardous plumes. Well-meaning but untrained people can become additional victims in a hazmat situation. If you suspect hazardous materials are involved, notify authorities and secure the site until trained responders can arrive. If there is threat of a fire or explosion, move back one-half mile. Some toxic chemicals require an even greater distance. Stay uphill, upwind, and upstream. Avoid contact with spills, fumes, vapors, and smoke. Even odorless fumes could be dangerous. If you become contaminated, notify authorities immediately, and they will assist in decontamination.

After Evacuation from a Hazmat Accident

- Do not return home until authorities say its safe.
- Open up windows and ventilate the house.
- If your house and yard are contaminated, be rigorous in following authorities' decontamination procedures. Contaminated shoes

could bring residue into your house. Contaminated clothes could contaminate your living spaces. Residue on the hands could be transferred to food or drink or other people.

- Hazardous material accidents in our communities are possible but usually small and isolated. Our local fire departments have extensive training and quick access to specialists if required. Be sure your family knows that individuals without training and equipment should not attempt to help with hazmat accidents. Families should be prepared to evacuate if authorities require.

Emergency preparedness:
Do one thing today.

WINTER

A Little Winter Weather Preparation Can Save You Grief

Every year, there are needless injuries and damage due to winter weather. With a little preparation, you can avoid many of the seasonal hazards.

Prepare Your House

- Inspect your furnace annually.

- Have a professional inspect the fuel system, fireboxes, and flues of older furnaces.

- Examine motor and belts for wear.

- Examine wiring for signs of overheating: cracking, discoloration.

- Clean or replace filters.

- Clear trash and combustible materials away from furnace and flue.

- Cover your evaporative cooler; stuff insulation into the cooler duct to reduce drafts. Make sure the water to the evaporative cooler is off and the supply line completely drained. Swamp cooler water lines can freeze in unheated attics and split, flooding insulation and ceilings.

- Replace door seals if ineffective. Install weather stripping. Install storm windows if you have them.

- Clean leaves out of gutters so melting roof snow can flow freely to the ground.
- Winterize your water pipes: caulk or stuff external wall penetrations. Insulate or heat trace exposed pipes and pipes in overhangs and unheated spaces. In extreme cold, let faucets drip to prevent freezing. If pipes freeze, do not use open flames to thaw. Wrap frozen area in rags and pour hot water over the rags.
- Make sure the main water shutoff is accessible.
- Routinely check all electrical cords for wear, and don't overload electrical circuits.
- Keep a fire extinguisher (or three) on hand. Check all smoke alarms (every level should have one or more).
- Keep fire hydrants clear of snow buildup.

Keep an Up-to-Date 72-Hour Kit

- Include: Water, food, extra blankets or sleeping bags, warm clothing, flashlight/batteries, candles/matches, radio/batteries, first-aid kit, personal toiletries, medications.
- Plan to have an emergency heating source:
  - » Fireplace or wood stove and fuel. (Do not use charcoal as an indoor heat source. It generates poisonous carbon monoxide.)
  - » Space heater and fuel. Always ensure adequate ventilation when operating a combustion heater.

Watch the Weather

- Be aware of approaching storms and plan your travel accordingly. Don't travel if you can avoid it. Allow extra time if you must travel.
- Make sure someone knows what route you are traveling and when you will arrive. Make sure your car is in good repair, and pack an emergency kit.
- Listen to weather updates on your radio during a storm.

Practice Fire Safety

- Check outside of fireplace or wood stove flues for adequate clearances and good repair.

- Check inside of fireplace or wood stove flues for creosote buildup. You may need to consult a professional.

- Protect fireplaces with screens. Keep young children away from space heaters.

- Provide adequate clearance between heater and combustible materials (thirty-six inches recommended).

- When running combustion heaters, provide adequate fresh air to prevent carbon monoxide buildup and oxygen starvation.

- Check kerosene heaters thoroughly each year. Make sure they have emergency shutoff valves in case heater is tipped over.

- Use only the specified fuel in space heaters, and follow all manufacturers' instructions.

- Store kerosene outside in approved metal containers.

- Never fill kerosene heaters when hot. Always refill outside.

- Clean out ashes only after they are completely cold. Discard ashes outside immediately in metal container.

- Make sure heaters and fires are out and cold before you go to sleep.

Dress for the Weather

- Watch the weather and avoid going out in extreme cold or blizzard conditions.

- Remember that wind can provide an extra danger to exposed flesh. Cover all skin in cases of extreme weather, even for short trips.

- Wear layers of loose clothing. The outer layer should be waterproof and windproof. The inner layer should be synthetic (not cotton) to wick moisture away from the body. Layers in between can be almost any insulating material.

- Keep dry. Getting wet in the winter can be life threatening. When you are wet, you lose much more body heat, and many materials lose their insulative properties.

- Good mittens will keep fingers warmer than gloves.

- Wear a hat covering the head down to the ears.

- Cover your mouth and nose with a scarf or bandanna in extreme cold.

Don't Overdo It

- Snow shoveling and car pushing are hard work. Stretch and warm up before any exertion. Rest frequently. Heart attacks injure more people than hypothermia.

- Try not to work up a sweat, especially if you do not have a refuge. When you finally slow down, you'll chill quickly if your clothing layers are soaked.

- Drink plenty of fluids. Winter air is dry, and you can dehydrate quickly.

- Watch slippery sidewalks.

- Don't forget to check regularly on neighbors during winter storms and harsh weather, especially the elderly or those with special needs. Sometimes those with poor circulation are not aware that they are becoming chilled.

As with other extreme situations, don't panic in a winter storm: the best preparedness tool you can have is your brain.

Tips for Winter Driving

Weather from October to April in snowy areas presents special challenges for drivers. Not only are roads more hazardous, but the consequences of getting stranded are more severe. Prepare your car now and use common sense when planning your travel.

Prepare Your Car for Winter Travel

- Make sure your car is in good operating condition.

- Check and winterize all systems. Pay special attention to your battery, the antifreeze, and wiper blades.

- Install snow tires or purchase chains.

- Keep a full gas tank, even for short trips. If stranded, you can run the heater longer.

Keep Up-to-Date Emergency Kits in the Car

- Start with a personal survival kit in the glove box:
  - » One large garbage sack to use as a poncho. Add a space blanket if you have one.

101

» Five or six quart-sized plastic sacks to use as expedient socks and gloves

» A one-gallon plastic sack can be used as a hat. But store a hat too.

» Hard candy for energy and morale

» A flashlight

» Waterproof matches and several candles for light and a little heat. Double-bag candles to prevent a mess if they melt in a too-warm car.

- Put other emergency gear in the back:
  » Ice scraper/brush
  » Blankets or sleeping bag
  » First-aid kit
  » Jumper cables
  » Extra food, high energy
  » Fire extinguisher
  » Tow strap
  » Distress flag
  » Basic tools
  » Hats, gloves, boots, socks
  » Plastic sheeting
  » Flares
  » Pocketknife
  » Shovel
  » Radio, batteries
  » Number 10 can with sealing lid (expedient toilet)
  » Salt/sand/kitty litter
  » Tissues

Plan Your Trip with the Weather in Mind

- Be aware of the weather on your route.

- Make sure someone knows of your destination, route, and planned arrival time. If conditions force you to change your plans, stop and call ahead.

- If you encounter weather that seems especially severe, seek shelter immediately. If it's just a brief flurry, you'll be back on your way soon. If it's a monster storm, you won't risk becoming stranded.

- Obey all road closures.

Use Common Sense When Driving

- Keep windows clear of snow, ice, and interior fogging.

- Allow extra time so you can adjust your speed to conditions.

- Anticipate ice on overpasses.

- Expect slippery conditions and anticipate the decisions of other drivers.

- Anticipate intersections. Brake slowly to avoid locking the wheels and losing control. If you start to skid, steer into the direction you want to go. Brake carefully.

If You Get Stranded

Every winter, severe storms strand cars on the road. Sometimes it can last a long and scary night. What should you do?

- Stay calm. If you panic, you lose your most important tool—your brain.

- Stay with the car. A car is more likely to be found when the inevitable search crews get out. You are much more likely to get lost, especially in a storm, if you leave the car. The car is shelter from the wind and protection from the snow, and it holds many tools and implements that you couldn't carry with you.

- Avoid overexertion. Avoid exposure. Stay in the car as much as possible. It may be possible to dig your car out of a drift, but it should be obvious after only a few minutes whether or not you should give it up. Avoid working up a sweat.

- If you try to push the car out, keep away from the wheels. Getting run over will not help your situation.

- Only run the motor for short periods. A good rule of thumb is ten to fifteen minutes per hour. Make absolutely sure that snow has not blocked the exhaust pipe, and crack a downwind window for ventilation. Remember that car exhaust can be just as fatal as freezing.

- Open doors and windows occasionally to get fresh air and to keep them from freezing shut. Keep a downwind window cracked if you burn a candle.

- Get out and clear off the car once in a while so it looks like a car and not a snow bank and is more visible to rescue crews.

- Exercise and stretch briefly, but vigorously, from time to time. Don't stay in one position too long.

- Don't allow everyone to sleep at once. Someone should keep a watch at all times.

- Use emergency flashers sparingly to conserve the battery, but use them as a signal at night. You may have to get out and clear the snow so they can be seen.

- Your car has many survival resources, so be innovative. The horn can be an effective signal. Use bursts of three, the universal distress signal. Be innovative in the use of car parts: a hubcap makes a crude snow scoop; seat insulation can be stripped out and stuffed into clothes; floor mats can be tied around feet; and so on.

Be Prepared to Have More Winter Fun

Winter is a great time to enjoy outdoor sports. Skiing, snowmobiling, snowshoeing, and even camping are all great ways to get out of the house, out of the smog, and into the stunning, snow-covered landscape. Because of weather extremes, however, minor mishaps in remote areas could become major disasters. Here are some preparation ideas to give you an extra margin of safety.

Prepare Yourself for Outdoor Activities

- Wear proper clothing. Wear layers of loose clothing. The outer layer should be waterproof and windproof. The inner layer should be synthetic (not cotton) to wick moisture away from the body. Layers in between can be almost any insulating material.

- Plan thoroughly and ask "what if?" Identify potential risks and then prepare for them. If you are not experienced at your planned activity, consult someone who is.

- Make sure someone knows of your destination, your route, and your time of return. Know the area—the landmarks, the routes to help and safety. Never travel in remote areas alone.

- Pay attention to the weather and plan (or delay) your trip accordingly.

- If you are using a vehicle like a snowmobile, make sure it is in good repair and you are adequately trained to operate it. Use all recommended safety precautions and operate it according to manufacturer's instructions. Many accidents occur when equipment is not used as designed.

- Learn the symptoms and treatment for cold injuries like hypothermia and frostbite. Hypothermia, for example, occurs when the body temperature drops, and it can ultimately be fatal. Hypothermia can occur even in mild weather. The first symptom is uncontrollable shivering, and steps must be taken immediately to get the victim warm.

- Keep an up-to-date emergency kit with you. Include:
  - » High-energy food, candy
  - » Candles/waterproof matches
  - » First-aid kit
  - » Extra socks, extra gloves, hat
  - » Space blanket, garbage sacks (forty-gallon), quart-sized baggies for hand/feet protection
  - » Whistle for signaling

If You Get Stranded

- Don't panic. Your best survival tool is your brain.

- If you are with a vehicle, like a car or snowmobile, consider staying with it, especially if it is dark or snowing. The vehicle is usually the first thing searchers find, and you can easily get disoriented in blowing snow. Make sure you know where you are going if you decide to travel.

- Keep fuel in your body so it can manufacture more heat. Don't be afraid to eat emergency food right away. Keep drinking; dehydration is a risk. Move vigorously from time to time when stranded, but don't work up a sweat.

Protect Your Body Heat

The body loses heat in five basic ways:

1. **Radiation:** Heat flows from warmer objects that are exposed to cooler objects. All of the heat of the sun comes to the earth by radiation. In the winter, any exposed area of your body will radiate heat to the snow, the air, or the sky. Those areas where blood vessels are close to the surface, such as heads and hands, are particularly vulnerable.

    The way to beat radiation loss is to "hide the heat." Cover everything up. Layers are especially important in thwarting radiation losses. Aluminized mylar "space blankets" (and bags) are specially designed to shield against radiation loss.

2. **Conduction:** When a warmer object contacts a cooler object, heat is transferred from the warmer. This is the kind of heat transfer that occurs when you are frying a hamburger in a pan.

    The way to beat conduction is to put insulation between the warmer (hopefully you) and cooler objects (like snow). Never sit or lay directly on the snow. If you have to sit, cut some tree branches or pile up some brush or leaves. Try to avoid eating large amounts of snow, since melting snow also takes heat.

3. **Evaporation:** Heat is consumed when moisture is evaporated. This is the principle on which swamp coolers are based. If your body heat is trying to dry out wet clothes, you can consume a lot of energy without getting warmer.

    The way to beat evaporation is to stay dry. Even sweating can be life threatening if you are caught out in the cold. Dress in layers that you can take off or loosen if you have to exert yourself. If you get wet while out, change to dry clothes if you have them. It is better to get out of wet things and into a blanket or sleeping bag than to wait for your clothes to dry. If you can't get out of wet stuff, try to insulate it with a large plastic garbage sack over everything except your face.

4. **Convection:** This is the type of heat loss that occurs when the wind is blowing: the wind chill factor. Air is a pretty good insulator when it is trapped between layers of clothing. But when the wind is blowing, your body will lose heat at a faster rate.

Convection can be beat by getting out of the wind or by covering up. Stay in the car, get behind a tree, get into a ditch (a dry ditch) or a snow cave, or hide behind a snow bank. And cover up all exposed skin. The large garbage sack is especially useful here.

5. **Respiration** (similar to evaporation): When you breathe, you take in cold, dry air and exhale wet, warm air. The whole process costs you heat. (Breathing takes heat, but it's better than the alternative.)

You can beat respiration loss by reducing the amount of exhaling, reducing your activity level. You can also beat it by breathing through your nose. This pre-warms the air before it comes into your lungs, and it captures a fraction of the heat and moisture that is in your breath when you exhale. Another tip is to breathe through a scarf or bandanna wrapped around your face. Again, this provides a little bit of pre-warming of intake air by capturing exhaled heat and moisture in the scarf. Only use fabric around your mouth and nose. Plastic is hazardous and will not be effective.

There is no need to avoid your favorite winter sports; just use a little common sense and a little preparation to make them more safe.

Emergency preparedness:
Do one thing today.

SUMMER

Surviving Extreme Heat

The United States has many desert regions that possess beauties and wonders all their own. With a flora and fauna specifically adapted to the uniquely harsh conditions, deserts are fascinating and captivating at any season. But, whether you are exploring on purpose or just passing through, extreme heat in a summer desert can be dangerous. Even nondesert climates and cities have heat waves that can prove fatal to vulnerable individuals. Here are a few tips to ensure more safety during summer fun or travel.

Know (and Avoid) the Effects of Heat

- Avoid dehydration. In the heat, your body constantly sweats, even when you don't feel damp. The constant drain of water eventually catches up; your blood gets thicker, and your heart has to work harder against increased pressure. When it has to work too hard, life-threatening complications can arise.

- Heat exhaustion is a form of hyperthermia, or elevated body temperature. The symptoms include cramps, headache, nausea, dizziness, confusion, irritability, excessive sweating, and cold and clammy skin.

- Heatstroke is a more serious injury. The symptoms include hot, dry skin; dry mouth; headache; nausea and vomiting; deep, rapid breathing; muscular twitching; and collapse.

In all cases, the victim should be cooled immediately and should take small amounts of water frequently, if conscious. Seek medical help immediately.

Protect Yourself When in the Sun, Even on Purpose

- Wear proper clothing: loose-fitting, lightweight, long-sleeved, light colors, cotton. Cotton clothes hold moisture close to you, lowering body temperature by evaporation.

- Wear a wide brim hat and good sunglasses with UV protection. Slather on the high-SPF sunscreen and don't forget lip protection. If you are on bright sand or reflecting water, put sunscreen under your chin and nose too.

- Drink a lot of water during summer activities, even before you feel thirsty. If highly active (working, running, biking, hiking), you might need two to four quarts an hour.

- If you plan on desert hiking or biking activities, study up on desert survival techniques and make sure you are equipped and prepared, even for an emergency. Take plenty of extra water and a dish if your dog is going with you, and watch the dog's feet carefully; hot sand and sharp rocks can take their toll.

Avoid Getting Stranded in Your Car

Follow similar guidelines for traveling in a desert as you do in the winter:

- Make sure your car is in good repair, especially the cooling system.
- Make sure your spare tire is in good shape and full of air.
- Travel on the full half of your gas tank.
- Tell someone your route and your expected arrival time.
- Stay on well-maintained roads; soft sand can strand you as easily as mud or snow.
- Carry an up-to-date emergency kit in your car that includes:
  - » Water for the car
  - » Extra belts
  - » Basic tools
  - » Tow chain

» Jumper cables

» Flares

» Shovel

» Fire extinguisher

» Water to drink

» Water purification tablets

» Plastic for solar still (6′ × 6′)

» High-energy food

» Blanket

» Matches

» Flashlight

» Radio and batteries

» First-aid kit

» Pocketknife

If Stranded in the Desert

- Stay calm.

- Stay out of the midday sun. Make your own shade if you have to.

- Consider staying with the car; it is more easily found, provides shelter, and contains many resources.

- Burn oil to make a smoky signal fire. Blinkers can be seen a long distance at night.

- Water is the main need if you are stranded in a desert. Make a solar still: dig a hole and place a clean pint- or quart-sized container in the bottom. Fill the hole with leaves and anything else that has moisture in it. Stretch a sheet of plastic over the hole and place a small rock on the sheet so that the low point hangs over the container. Try to keep the bottom side of the plastic clean. Drinking water will condense on it and flow to the cup. Make sure the plastic seals the hole airtight and you could get up to a quart of water in a day. Each time you open and reseal the hole it will take a couple of hours to start producing water again.

- Look for animal tracks or circling birds to guide you to nearby water sources. Follow the instructions on your water purification tablets to make the water safe to drink.

- Don't leave the car if you don't know exactly where you are going. If you have to travel, go in the cool mornings and evenings. Remember that no matter how hot the day, the nights could get chilly.

Beat the Heat with Common Sense

When we experience a combination of high heat and reduced power in the city, things get miserable quickly. Here are some tips to beat a heat wave in the city:

- Stay out of the heat. Move to your basement if you have one. Run a fan if there is electricity—moving air helps you stay cooler.

- Get enough to drink. Drink a little all of the time, even before you are thirsty. If your urine gets darker, drink more. Avoid all alcohol and caffeinated drinks; they flush water from your system.

- Eat smart and have balanced meals. Go for no-cook meals—they don't add heat to your house. Be sure to get enough salt and potassium (bananas or sports drinks—check the label).

- Rest a lot. Don't do any more strenuous activities than required. Hard work costs you two to four quarts of water per hour. Drugs such as antihistamines and thyroid medications can interfere with your body's ability to cool itself—check with your doctor before any strenuous activities.

- Wear loose-fitting clothes and a wide brim hat for all outdoor activities.

- Make sure your pets get plenty of water too.

- Heat waves are especially hard on the elderly. Check frequently on your neighbors during long hot spells. Offer to do some of their outdoor chores. Invite them to your cool house if theirs is hot or they can't afford to keep an air conditioner running. Encourage them to drink plenty.

Emergency preparedness:
Do one thing today.

POWER OUTAGE

When the Lights Go Out

When the lights go out, every toy on the floor becomes a hazard. Every piece of furniture becomes an obstacle. All activities cease while you try to remember the last place you saw the flashlight. Does it work? Does it have batteries? Are all the pieces even in one place? Once you find the light, everybody wants to use it to search for other lights or to continue whatever activity they were engaged in when the lights went out. A power failure is always inconvenient but rarely life threatening by itself. It can, however, lead to disorientation, injuries, and panic. Here are a few tips for preparing for the lights to go out.

Keep one flashlight in an easy-to-get-to, easy-to-find location. You have to be able to find this flashlight by touch, so know its exact location. Designate this flashlight as the no-kidding emergency light and threaten severe consequences to anyone who even thinks about using it for some other project or game. Buy some inexpensive lights for other uses so your emergency light stays put. Make sure your no-kidding emergency light is a good flashlight. It should have a large, bright beam and take standard batteries and bulbs. Buy an extra bulb or two and keep a spare set of batteries in another easy-to-find location. Some people like the rechargeable flashlights that plug into the wall because they are always ready and always in the same place. The hand-generator flashlights will do in a pinch, but all that squeezing gets tiring very quickly, so make sure it is not your only option.

The purpose of the no-kidding emergency light is to enable you to find and set up other light sources. It's a good idea to have more than one emergency source of light. You have many options:

- **Other flashlights**: In the past few years, a lot of good flashlight options have come on the market. We have an array of solid, well-engineered, and energy-miser options. LED lights lead the pack here. Be prepared to spend a little bit extra to get a flashlight that is sturdy and reliable. Look in outdoor stores for options that are hands-free (headlamps), water resistant, or have extra-bright or extra-wide beams. I suggest getting flashlights that are only flashlights and not attached to some other appliance. Get some extras for everyone in the family. Make sure the batteries are a common size and easily found.

- **Battery-powered lantern**: For area lighting, this is the safest choice, without a doubt. The main drawback is the cost of replacing batteries. If you use a battery-powered lantern often for camping, you might find it less expensive to invest in rechargeable batteries and a charger. LED options have been developed here too, so now might be a good time to upgrade.

- **Propane lantern**: Because there is a flame, these lanterns require considerably more supervision than battery-powered devices. Keep matches and lanterns out of the reach of children, and *never leave any open flame unattended*! Keep a window open for fresh air. Propane lanterns are convenient and have become less expensive in the past few years. The propane bottles are easy to store safely. Also store some extra mantles, and make sure you know where to find the matches. Although many families have the old white gas lantern hanging around, I would not recommend its use. The white gas lanterns have a liquid fuel that you must also store (in an approved safety container and outside of the house and garage), and refilling can be messy and dangerous.

- **Candles**: Candles are inexpensive, readily available, and good for long-term storage. Again, because of the open flame, candles should never be left unattended or in the care of children. Tall, thin candles are unstable and require a candleholder. Dripping wax can leave a mess, and if it splashes on your hand, you might be surprised into dropping the candle, creating a fire hazard. Tub candles and tea candles are more stable and less likely to drip wax, and you can buy candle lanterns to hold them and protect the flame from the draft. Be careful, though—candle lanterns can get very hot on top. For a little more expense, you can get a backpacker's candle lantern, which uses a longer-lasting candle and is designed for efficiency.

- **Kerosene lamp:** Several kerosene lamps are popular, including the hurricane lantern and the "Aladdin" lamp. Observe proper fire safety rules, and you'll need to crack open a window for fresh air. These larger light sources also give off considerable heat but some-times leave a kerosene smell. It's a good idea to store an extra wick, some extra mantles, and even an extra glass chimney. You'll also need to store kerosene. Use an approved safety container and keep out of reach of children.

- **Chemical sticks:** These don't give much light, but they can be seen from a long distance away and are quite safe. Some commercial vendors tout light sticks as a good light source if you suspect a gas leak, but the best advice if you suspect a gas leak is to leave the house immediately until professionals can fix the problem.

After you have prepared for a power outage, have a lights-out prac-tice or two, either preannounced or pop quiz style, to make sure every-one knows what to do. Make it fun for the kids by fixing a snack or playing games, and they might even develop a positive attitude about emergency preparedness.

An Extended Power Outage Can Test Your Preparedness

Think for a minute of all the ways electricity touches your life: the alarm clock to wake you up, the lights that illuminate your predawn house, the refrigerator that keeps your food from spoiling, the range or stove for cooking breakfast, the furnace blower to heat your house, the automatic garage door opener to let the car out, the gas pumps at the filling station, the traffic lights on the road, the cash registers at the grocery store, the computer on your desk at work, the TV, the radio, the stereo, the can opener, the water softener, the iron, and on and on. And that doesn't count the zillion devices that we use all day and recharge all night: phones, tablet computers, electronic readers. Our lives are so dependent upon electricity that it's hard to imagine being without it. But there are many scenarios that could deprive us of this convenience for a long time. Superstorm Sandy in 2012 brought high winds that took down trees and power lines with them. It was such a large storm—over a thousand miles across—that the damage covered a large area, and repair crews were stretched to find and fix all of the outages. Most of the people affected by Sandy were without power for three to five days. But a significant number were without power for days longer and, in some cases, weeks. Sandy also highlighted the vulnerability of the aging power infrastructure. An accident or terrorist act at a major power plant or two and large areas would be without electricity for an extended period.

While short-term power outages are frequent enough that we don't worry about getting through them, long-term outages could really test our emergency preparations. Life without electricity is very different from normal—it takes more time, more effort, and all of your patience to do anything. An outage of a few minutes or a few hours can be annoying (you always forget how many clocks and timers have to be reset), but life in an extended power outage is vastly different.

Several years ago, elementary and secondary school children from New England shared their thoughts about the good and bad aspects of their extended power outage. Many of them commented on meeting new people at the shelter, doing things other than watching TV like reading, talking to family, playing games in front of the fireplace, having dinner by candlelight, and partying with neighbors when it was over. But they also noted that there were hard parts too, like stinky toilets, carrying water for flushing, food spoiling in the refrigerator, damage to houses and cars, soot and smoke in the house from emergency heaters, and boredom.

So what do you do if there is a power outage? First, check to see if any of your neighbors have lights. If your nearest neighbors have power, then you need to look at your own fuse or circuit breaker box. Disconnect or turn off large appliances first. Check the main breaker; if it is tripped, turn it off and then on. Then turn on lights and appliances one at a time and see if the breaker trips again. If it does, it could indicate a faulty appliance or an overloaded circuit. If you are uncertain what to do or can't find the problem, call an electrician. If you have a fuse box with screw-in fuses, a blackened fuse window indicates a blown fuse. If you have cartridge fuses, many of them give no indication when they blow. You'll need to check them with an ohmmeter or call an electrician. If you find a fuse blown because of overload, *do not replace it with a larger fuse*! This is often the cause of electrical fires. Shift some lights or appliances to another circuit.

If the electrical outage is widespread, turn on your battery-powered or hand-cranked radio to find out how widespread and how long it is predicted to last. What you do next depends on what season it is. In the winter, you'll need to make a decision about staying in your home or evacuating to a friend's house or a heated shelter. This will likely depend on whether you have a heat source or not. Just because the power goes out does not mean that the gas goes out. But even if you have gas, the electricity to blowers will be missing. You may need an alternate heat source. A fireplace or wood stove with a good wood supply, or a kerosene heater, gives you some options to stay home in extreme weather. In the summer, you may still need to decide if you'll go to a shelter in extreme weather, but exposure is less of an issue.

A few words about generators: in Sandy, generators, fuel, and replacement parts were scarce commodities. If you choose to invest in a generator—and they can be pricey—be sure to do your homework. How much power will you need? You will not be able to replace your entire house service, but you might be able to run your furnace fan or your freezer for a few hours a day. Well before an emergency, have an electrician help you figure out if you can connect your generator into your house panel and exactly how to do it safely. Practice it often enough that you can do it under trying circumstances, like dark or cold. Be sure you properly store fuel and spare parts. Estimate how much fuel you might need and get a little extra. Remember, you are not trying to maintain your pre-outage lifestyle—you are trying to survive. Also, generators account for a significant fraction of deaths and injuries, so follow all safety precautions, especially those about only running it outdoors and managing the exhaust so it doesn't get back into the house.

You'll also have to pay attention to your freezer and refrigerator. A full freezer with good door seals will keep food safely frozen for about two days, less if the door is opened often. Extra space in the freezer or poor seals will reduce the time. If the weather is below freezing, you can put frozen goods in secure containers (animal protection) and place them outside. Note: after a power outage, examine your frozen foods—they may be safely refrozen if they still contain ice crystals or if they remain below forty degrees. Use refrozen foods as soon as possible.

If in doubt, throw it out; risking your health isn't worth a few pennies of food.

In Winter

- Bundle up in layers that you can add and remove as you warm and chill.

- Stay moderately active to produce body heat. Don't work up a sweat.

- If you have a fireplace or other temporary heat source, open cabinets under sinks to get the warmed air to the water pipes. If your house is unheated and temperatures are significantly below freezing, you may want to drain water pipes or put antifreeze in undrainable traps. Note: Antifreeze is toxic and should not be put into drinking-water pipes.

- Drink lots of water—dehydration is a cold weather risk—and eat hearty meals for energy.

In Summer

- Your refrigerator and freezer will warm up much more quickly. Eat cool foods as soon as possible. Don't take any chances with spoiled food.

- Drink lots of liquids and eat balanced meals.

Tips from Sandy Survivors that are Applicable In Any Outage

- Keep your 72-hour kit up to date. Be sure it contains a manual can opener.

- Keep lanterns and flashlights in working order—it's tougher to service a flashlight after the lights go out, and stores (if they open at all without power) may sell out of lights and batteries first. If you live in a high-rise building, your elevators will not work, and stairwells rarely have windows; you'll need a good flashlight just to get out to the street.

- Store cash. ATMs and credit card machines may not work, even if stores have supplies.

- Don't tough out a power outage alone. Check on neighbors, especially the elderly or the ill.

- You need a lot more food than you think if it is cold and especially if everyone is out of school and home from work all day. But all of the food in the world won't help you if it is inedible. Store what you eat. And store some extra: will you really be able to turn away your children's friends?

- Make sure you have enough toilet paper. Enough said.

- Store some luxury and comfort items too. You'll need that reward after a few days.

- In the winter, it gets dark early. Nights can be really long. Store some cards, store some games, and keep your guitar in tune.

- The power company recommends you turn off appliances and lights and turn them on one at a time when service is restored. This avoids a large load on the system when the power finally comes back on and helps prevent another immediate power failure.

- Don't try to beat it by yourself—go out to dinner if the rest of town has power. Take your friend up on his offer to let you use his shower. And if you are the friend with the shower, offer it to your friends.

- You can still cook outdoors on a gas or charcoal grill, but do not bring the device into an enclosed space to cook; gases from incomplete combustion are deadly.

- Store some paper plates and utensils. They conserve water, and cleanup is easier.

- Pay attention to electrical appliances you use for personal grooming—electric razor, curlers, curling iron, and so on—and make nonelectrical arrangements if these devices are essential to your well-being.

- Get an extra charging cord for your phone. Get two, and keep one handy all of the time; you never know when you will find a socket with power to charge your device for a few critical minutes.

- Although public safety folks tell us that a traffic light outage means a four-way stop, to many it might mean a "no-way stop." Drive defensively.

- Remember: Everyone around you is also at his or her breaking point. After Hurricane Sandy, there were fights over fuel and supplies.

- Be patient. Realize that even simple chores without utilities are harder and more time intensive.

Emergency preparedness:
Do one thing today.

HIGH WINDS,
TORNADOES, HURRICANES

When the Wind Blows

When you think of high winds, you probably think of the extreme winds of hurricanes along the Gulf and Atlantic coasts. Perhaps you think of tornadoes with their short-lived but destructive winds. While these are certainly the storms that get the most attention, virtually all parts of the country are vulnerable to high winds of some kind: hurricanes, tornadoes, thunderstorms/microbursts, or other extreme conditions. The result is often the same—houses are damaged, trees are broken and downed, utilities are interrupted for hours or days. Sometimes there are even injuries and deaths. Whatever the cause, here are a few things you can do to minimize the impact of a wind storm.

Before a wind storm, you should make sure that your 72-hour kit is complete, current, and available. Every six months or so, you should review the contents of your kit and replace time-sensitive items like medications, water, and some foods. Make sure that batteries are fresh and that clothing fits.

Staying informed of weather conditions is also important. Meteorologists can predict the conditions that lead to wind-producing storm systems and will issue watches and warnings when conditions require. Current weather conditions are broadcast on NOAA weather radios, public radio stations, or TV, so your 72-hour kit should contain a battery-powered radio and fresh batteries, in case the power goes out.

If you have sufficient warning, prepare your house and yard. Bring in the trash cans, lawn furniture, and other loose items that can become destructive missiles. All throughout the year, you should pay attention to your yard, remove old or unbalanced trees, and trim dead branches and those close to utility lines. In hurricane country, it would be wise to have plywood window covers already cut to install quickly. In tornado country, you will need to find or build a tornado shelter.

During a windstorm, stay indoors if possible. If roof-mounted swamp coolers or antennas become loose during a windstorm, it is safest to let the storm abate before getting on the roof to assess damage and start repairs. If you must go out in the storm, avoid downed power lines. If you see one, always assume that it is live and stay away. If you must drive, watch for debris on the roads. Also remember that intersections with traffic lights become four-way stops if the power is out. When in doubt, yield the right-of-way. Of course high-profile vehicles like campers, RVs, and some panel trucks and lightly loaded trailers are at risk in high winds.

Tornadoes in the South and Midwest

Every year in the United States, over 1,250 tornadoes touch down, although in extreme years, it can be closer to 1,800. They leave trails from a hundred feet to hundreds of yards wide, and from a few blocks to miles long. About sixty people die each year in tornadoes. Although tornadoes are reported in all months and all states, most tornadoes occur between the first of March and the end of August. In the United States, most tornadoes occur in Nebraska, Kansas, Oklahoma, and Texas, although they occur in almost all states. Most tornado damage and destruction comes from high winds and flying debris. Occasionally lightning strikes and locally low atmospheric pressures cause damage.

Preparation consists primarily of staying alert to weather conditions, having a plan for seeking safe shelter, and having a 72-hour kit current and available. When officials issue a tornado watch, it means that tornadoes are possible. A tornado warning means that a tornado has been sighted. If you see a tornado, or if officials direct you, go to your safe shelter. In a house or small building, go to the basement or storm cellar. If there is no basement, seek an interior room, closet, or hallway—a room without windows—on the lowest level. Get under a sturdy table and protect yourself from flying debris by covering with a quilt or mattress. Stay put until the danger has passed. Mobile homes are not safe in tornadoes, even if anchored. Seek shelter in a permanent structure.

When Do Tornadoes Happen?

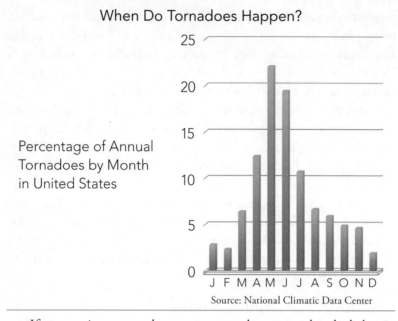

Percentage of Annual
Tornadoes by Month
in United States

Source: National Climatic Data Center

If you are in a car and you see a tornado, stop and seek shelter in a nearby building if there is one. If you are in a car on the road and you get hit by flying debris, pull over, park, and leave your seat belt on. Try to get your face below the window level and cover yourself with a blanket or coat. If you can clearly see that you can safely get lower than the level of the road, leave the car and seek shelter in a ditch or low spot that doesn't have power lines running over it. Don't go under a bridge or overpass. Lie face down and put your hands over your head. A culvert may not be a safe choice if there is rain since flash flooding is more dangerous and more likely than the tornado itself.

In a public place, go to the designated shelter area. If no area is designated, go to an interior, glassless room on the lowest floor. Stay out of elevators since power outages are common. Avoid wide-span roofs like auditoriums, theaters, and gyms. A smaller room without windows like a bathroom, an office, or a maintenance closet would be a safer place to ride out the danger.

After the tornado, use caution getting around. Downed power lines and foot hazards like broken glass and debris may abound. Wear heavy gloves and work boots for cleanup. It is estimated that fifty percent of tornado-related injuries occur after the tornado has passed. Also, keep tuned to the weather news since tornadoes are often spawned in a weather front that may be able to continue to affect you.

Hurricanes along the Gulf and Atlantic Coasts

Hurricanes are a real threat, but they are much larger and more predictable storms than tornadoes. Forecasters are now able to give two to five days notice of an impending hurricane and its predicted path, so pay attention to weather conditions.

Hurricane Katrina and Superstorm Sandy showed clearly that you should leave when authorities say you should leave and maybe even sooner. Don't stay in harm's way. Board up and move inland as soon as possible. Although the winds and the battering rain are damaging, the storm surge—the huge dome of sea water blown ashore by the storm—is historically far more dangerous and far more damaging than the wind. Moving away from the coast takes you out of the way of the storm surge. Heavy rains also make inland flooding a possibility, so stay away from low-lying or flood-prone areas.

It is important to evacuate to a safe area early to avoid traffic jams and road closures due to storm or debris. Key to a swift evacuation is a streamlined checklist for securing the home or business. Make sure that you know exactly what preparations you want to make and that you have the materials on hand. For example, permanent storm shutters or precut plywood sheets ($5/8$-inch marine grade) will greatly speed window protection. Tape will not prevent windows from breaking. Secure outdoor furniture. Fuel your car. If you practice driving the evacuation route occasionally, it will be familiar in the stress of an emergency. When evacuating, take your 72-hour kits and all of the extra water you can. Make plans about where you will reunite if separated. Use your designated out-of-state contact to facilitate communication with your family.

After a hurricane, stay tuned to TV or radio to find out about special conditions and emergency responses that may apply to your area. Return home only when officials say it is safe. If you cannot return home and need to find a shelter, text SHELTER and then your zip code (for example, SHELTER 12345) to 4FEMA (43362) to find the nearest shelter.

Realize that flooding may have contaminated food and water sources and take proper hygienic precautions. During recovery efforts, pay attention to the warning signs of stress, exhaustion, and fatigue and pace yourself accordingly. Heart attacks kill too.

• • •

High wind emergency preparedness, whether for tornadoes in Kansas or hurricanes in Florida, consists mainly of paying attention to the weather and keeping a disaster supplies kit current and available for quick evacuation. This is good advice for almost all emergencies, anyway.

Emergency preparedness:
Do one thing today.

FLOODS

Climate Change, Unexpectedly Extreme Weather

Over the past several years, scientists have linked increases in atmospheric "greenhouse gases" to an increasing temperature trend: global warming. Scientific studies have proliferated, and the debate has become heated, no pun intended. It is not my intent to join the debate on why the climate is warming but to discuss the implications for your family's preparedness.

No matter the cause, the data indicate that global temperatures are rising. When this effect is added to normal climate and weather variations, such as El Niño/La Niña (seasonally warmer and cooler water off the western coast), and just the random variability in weather patterns, it seems to predict more extreme weather. There are several possible effects:

- Warmer oceans deliver more moisture and energy to the atmosphere, resulting in bigger, more powerful storms, affecting more people, more often.

- Melting polar ice will increase sea levels, thereby increasing flood risks for more people along populous coasts.

- Changes in weather patterns mean that some regions will be surprised by either much hotter or much colder extremes than history has prepared them for.

- Long-term changes in climate patterns can result in flooding in some places and drought in others.

Scientists don't know specifics. Will winter in Des Moines be harsher or milder than usual? Will the spring rains in Texas be heavier or lighter than usual? Will there be more hurricanes and twisters or fewer? The prediction technology is not accurate enough to tell.

But in preparedness terms, this uncertainty is not different from any other season or any other year. In fact, the potential for severe weather is always with us. If the climate wasn't warming and changing, could we let our guard down? Probably not—basic family preparedness principles are the same, with or without climate change. If there are more extreme winter storms, respond as you learned in chapter 15. If there are more power outages because of more high winds, respond as you learned in chapters 17 and 18. Climate change may be happening, but it won't change how your family prepares.

Seasonal Flooding

In many parts of the world, spring means floods. Although higher elevations like the Mountain States do not have as much risk of the types of floods that inundate large river valleys, there are still any number of ways individual homes can be flooded, from inside or from out.

Before a Flood

Know the Risks

- Drainages, from local rivers to neighborhood ditches, can receive more spring melt and storm runoff than they can handle. FEMA continually updates flood risk maps that cover the entire United States and show where flooding can be expected (http://www.fema. gov/national-flood-insurance-program/map-service-center).

- A high water table can flood homes from beneath. Water tables rise and fall seasonally.

- Homes in colder climates have some risk of pipes freezing and bursting. A cold spell coupled with a power outage could mean trouble for pipes in outside walls.

- Even a small plumbing leak in any weather can cause problems. One family came back after a summer vacation to find an upstairs leak had flooded all of the levels below. The ceilings collapsed; standing water ruined walls and furniture. The house had to be completely refinished.

- A small amount of soil settling near your foundation can allow thunderstorm runoff from the roof to puddle near the house or run into window wells, flooding basements.

- City storm drains, if plugged with dirt or debris, can back up and flood nearby property.

Know Your Insurance Coverage

- A typical homeowner's policy covers flooding originating within the home (like broken pipes, overflowing fixtures, and so on) but does not cover flooding from outside. External flood insurance usually requires an additional policy or endorsement. When you apply for flood insurance (talk to your agent about options and costs), the company will inspect your property or consult a FEMA map to determine if you are in a high-risk area for flooding, or "floodplain." If you are, flood coverage could cost more. Assess the risks to your property to determine whether you should spend your money mitigating the flooding risks or investing in insurance.

- Make sure the policy pays replacement value for your possessions; otherwise, your reimbursement will be depreciated to current value and may not allow you to replace everything at today's prices. Raising the deductible limit—the amount you pay before the insurance coverage takes over—reduces premium costs.

- Inventory your possessions with lists, photographs, videos, and receipts. Make a copy and put this information, along with insurance policies, in a watertight container in safe place. Store the original in a safe-deposit box or other off-site location.

Prepare Now to Minimize Future Damage

- Make drainage modifications to your property before it rains. Put extensions on downspouts to get roof water away from the house. Use decorative berms and raised gardens to channel water or provide a few extra inches of flood protection.

- Keep storm drains and culverts near your house free of debris.

- Insulate pipes against freezing. Pipes in outside walls are most vulnerable.

- Protect valuable papers, books, photos, and heirlooms. Store them in watertight plastic tubs. Store them off the floor on shelves or pallets.

- Everyone in the family should know where all utility shutoffs are. Visibly mark shutoffs so a friend or neighbor can find them easily.

- When you go on a trip, have a trusted neighbor regularly check your house inside and out. Then someone has access to your house if there is an emergency while you are gone.

During a Flood

- Stay out of floodwater. Water only inches deep can be swift and unbalancing. Floodwater can also be full of sewage, oil, gasoline, or chemicals. Do not drive through flooded areas.

- Be prepared to evacuate. Prepare a 72-hour kit for quick action and keep a list of other things you want to grab when the time comes.

- Follow instructions from local authorities. Flood situations can deteriorate rapidly.

- Shut off electricity in a flooded home until you are sure there is no electrocution hazard.

- Pilot lights in furnaces and water heaters can be extinguished by floodwater, requiring the gas valve be shut off.

After a Flood

- Make recovery efforts safe. Stay out of germ-laden floodwaters, wear gloves and safety glasses/goggles, and wash hands frequently. Discard food that has come in contact with floodwater. Be aware of electrocution hazards. Wear sturdy boots and gloves.

- Carefully examine your home for damage. Check for structural damage to the foundation and bearing walls. Inspect for gas leaks, pipe damage, and unsafe electrical situations.

- Listen for warnings about drinking tap water, which could be temporarily contaminated.

- Damp conditions can cause fungus growth, which aggravates asthma and allergies.

- Inventory your damaged possessions. Take pictures and make notes. Keep detailed records of cleanup costs for insurance claims.

- Professional disaster recovery companies can assist in rapid recovery with manpower and heavy duty equipment. Insurance companies often accept their damage assessments without question. Make sure you know if your policy covers their services.

- Freeze valuable wet books and papers as cold as possible, as soon as possible. Restoration experts have a better chance of saving them later.

- If water has sat in your home for any length of time, you will likely have to demolish all of the interior finish: carpets, flooring, walls.

- Be aware of stress, exhaustion, and the tendency to try to do everything at once. Realize that recovery may take many days or weeks. Eat well and rest often.

Hurricane Storm Surge

Another type of flooding associated with always-extreme hurricanes is storm surge. As dramatic and frightening as the wind of a hurricane can be, and as intimidating as the fierce rains can be, the storm surge of a hurricane is by far the most deadly and the most damaging to property. In the northern hemisphere, tropical storms and hurricanes slowly swirl in a counterclockwise direction. Because hurricanes form and strengthen at sea, the high winds push up a dome of seawater ahead of them, on the right-hand side when seen from a satellite. The sea level can rise up to twenty feet above normal, depending on the location, and can span hundreds of miles of coastline, so it is important to pay attention to the path of the center of the storm, where the winds will be highest, but also pay attention to coastal areas to the east and the north of the point of landfall. These are the areas vulnerable to storm surge. Storm surges add to the normal tides, so a combination of high tide and storm surge can be quite damaging. Superstorm Sandy came ashore in southern New Jersey, and the accompanying storm surge devastated a long shoreline from New Jersey through New York and even farther north. The high waves eroded beaches, and the surge overtopped breakwaters and levees built to withstand smaller storms.

Local and federal governments place beach dunes, rock barriers, and levees to protect communities, but they are not foolproof, and each installation has its limits of protection. And as ocean levels rise and storms become larger, what might have been adequate fifty years ago may not protect you today. Engineered shoreline protections can be defeated by a high surge, allowing water to destroy houses, roads, and utilities and to compromise sewage treatment plants, underground (and aboveground) fuel tanks, and hazardous material storage. Much of the densely populated Atlantic and Gulf Coast coastlines have an elevation less than ten feet above mean sea level, so the potential for destruction is high.

You can avoid storm surge by knowing where it is likely to happen and avoiding purchasing property there. FEMA's flood maps assess flooding and storm surge risks, so your realtor and your insurance agent can help you check it out. But there is a great attraction to the seashore, and many houses have been in families for generations. So if you own shore property, just realize that there are times it may not be protected.

The best thing—really, the only thing—to do when you are in the path of a storm surge is to evacuate. In Sandy, some people tried to "ride it out" to protect their homes, but their homes were still devastated, and they and their rescuers were needlessly endangered. And some died. So when authorities warn you to leave, leave. You should have a couple of days' notice to grab your 72-hour kits and other supplies and get to that inland location.

Before you leave, move furniture and items you want to save to an upper floor. Turn off the electricity and water. Authorities may also instruct you to turn off the gas. If you do, you will need to get the gas company to come turn it back on after the storm. If the damage has been widespread, that could take days.

After the storm has passed, only go to your home when authorities say the water has receded and it is safe. Your basement may be full of water, mud, and sand and will likely need to be gutted. Stay out of the water and wear gloves and glasses or goggles if you have to work near it; the water is likely to be full of stuff you don't want on your skin or in your eyes. While putting your life back together, pace yourself, eat right, and drink plenty of water, no matter the season. Obey instructions about what to do with waste and debris so you don't create another problem outside of your house.

• • •

Climate change and extreme weather may cause flooding problems, but the principles of preparation don't change—do what you can before the storm to minimize damage, get out of the way of the storm and the flooding, and use caution and common sense to recover.

Emergency preparedness:
Do one thing today.

TECHNOLOGICAL EMERGENCIES

Technology Risks

Technology pervades our lives, from the communications and utilities that we use every day to the interdependent systems that keep stores supplied with goods and financial systems working. Technology is responsible for much of the comfort we enjoy. But like anything else, it can go wrong. Technological emergencies are related to those things around us that are man-made, as opposed to natural phenomena such as tornadoes and hurricanes. For example, they may include

- Utility failure (see chapter 17 for a power outage)

- Hazardous materials incident (see chapter 14 for preparation and response)

- Chemical plant or refinery emergency

- Nuclear power plant emergency

- Widespread computer failure, whether from viruses or from solar storms

Chemical Plant or Refinery Emergency

There are many locations that produce, handle, or store hazardous materials. Some of them are close to homes and schools. The vast majority of them are regulated and safe. In some cases, though, it is difficult to separate fact from noise to determine whether a real danger exists. How do you know if a facility near you is under control or is an accident waiting to happen? Federal law provides citizens with the right to know about the dangers in their communities. Learning whether a facility is safe may be as simple as asking a few questions: What hazardous materials are involved? What processes are used? Where else has the process been tested? What happens to the wastes? What are the emergency plans? When are they tested? Who is in charge in an emergency? How are nearby residents alerted? Are there any unresolved legal or enforcement actions? If the answers to any of these questions are unsatisfactory, you can continue to ask them of facility officials or local, state, and federal authorities until you are satisfied with the answers.

Emergencies may consist of an airborne chemical plume mixed with steam or smoke, or a liquid spill that may be transported by sewers; storm drains; or natural creeks, rivers, and drainages. As part of preparing for such emergencies, communities may have established local emergency planning committees (LEPCs), who compile appropriate information about hazardous materials producers, transporters, storage facilities, and users in the area. LEPCs may also have prepared plans—including ways to notify the public and actions people must take to deal with such emergencies. Contact your local public safety authorities, such as local governments or fire departments, to find out what planning has been done. The information should be public.

In such incidents, you must avoid contact with, or inhalation or ingestion of, potentially harmful chemicals. As in other hazardous materials incidents (chapter 14), the public may be required to evacuate or to shelter in place. Sheltering in place amounts to staying put in your home while reducing the intake of outside air for a short duration while an airborne plume passes over. Your LEPC or public safety officials will tell you if it is a possibility for you, depending on the proximity of potential sources, and how to do it. You will likely be asked to keep some plastic sheeting, scissors, and duct tape in your emergency kit so you can seal off an interior room in which to stay for a short time, as needed. Other responses to chemical or refinery accidents may include restrictions on sources of fresh fruits, vegetables, livestock, and other foods from the potentially affected areas, depending on the chemical and the amount spilled.

Nuclear Power Plant Emergency

Nuclear power plants produce about one-fifth of the nation's electricity by converting the heat of fission reactions to steam to turn generator turbines. There are several types and designs of reactors, and design, construction, and operations of nuclear power plants are overseen by the Nuclear Regulatory Commission (NRC). Despite rigorous regulation, extensive monitoring, and an enviable safety record overall, a generation of experience has taught us that accidents can happen, releasing potentially dangerous amounts of radioactivity into our environment. FEMA estimates that about three million Americans live within a ten-mile radius of a nuclear power plant.

The unique hazard with nuclear power plants is exposure to radiation, and the primary transport mechanism of concern to the public is through the air in a plume of steam or smoke. People exposed to the plume might receive radiation directly through the plume or particles that deposit, or "fall out," of the plume, or through inhalation of airborne particles. Of course, there are natural and daily sources of radiation such as X-ray machines, TVs, and microwave ovens, but radiation is cumulative, and a nuclear accident could increase our dose past safe limits.

Protection from radiation is based upon time and distance. The longer a person is exposed to a higher dose of radiation, the more serious the effects. The farther away you can get, the smaller the dose; most forms of radiation drop off sharply after just a short distance. Distance can be effectively enhanced by placing more mass between you and the source as well. Time also plays a part, since radioactive materials decay over time. Some decay quickly in days or weeks, but there are some radioactive materials that persist for many years.

The key thing to know about nuclear accidents is the NRC requires operators to define two emergency planning zones to focus their response in case of an accident. Federal, state, and local governments all get involved. The first zone covers the area within a ten-mile radius of the reactors, which is at highest risk from direct exposure to radiation. The second zone expands to a fifty-mile radius where radioactive materials could get into the environment, water supplies, and food chain. Plant operators share these plans with state and local officials, who then prepare their response plans to protect the public in case of an accident. Regulations require a large-scale practice every two years to make sure the plans stay up-to-date, are workable, and are effective.

In case of an accident, authorities may require evacuation, or they may request you shelter in place. If you live within ten miles of a power plant, you should annually receive emergency preparation information from the power plant of your local emergency officials. These materials will tell you if you might be asked to shelter in place, and how to do it. As with similar emergencies, you will likely be asked to keep some plastic sheeting, scissors, and duct tape in your emergency kit so you can seal off an interior room in which to stay. Other responses to nuclear accidents may include restrictions on sources of fresh fruits, vegetables, livestock, and other foods from the potentially affected areas. If you have any questions, call your local officials or the state department of public safety.

Widespread Computer Failure

Toward the end of 1999, there was much concern about a potentially widespread computer programming glitch where the use of two-digit codes for years would result in a lot of confused computers when the new year turned over to 1/1/2000 (year 2000 or "Y2K"), potentially wreaking havoc on our computerized world. There was a flurry of activity to reprogram everything from social security payment computers to coffee machines. In the end, whether because of the preparation or in spite of it, there was not much disruption, not much confusion, and certainly no havoc. But Y2K did highlight how dependent we are on computers and embedded chips, and how thoroughly everything from factory processes to just-in-time transportation systems to medical care could be turned upside down if it all goes wrong at the same time. Although a Y2K-like glitch is not on the horizon, after thirteen years our vulnerability to a widespread failure of computers is more profound than ever. How might a widespread computer failure be triggered? Hacking and malware (viruses), and—though less likely—solar flares.

- **Hacking:** For reasons I do not understand, there are people in the world who try to interrupt, disrupt, and corrupt everyone else's computer through viruses, Trojans, spam attacks, and so on. Many viruses are fairly innocuous and focused more at stealing personal information or hooking your computer into their network of "spambots." But more malignant types of hacking are certainly out there: the hacker who wants to make a name and reputation; the hacker that is protesting some real or perceived injustice; the state-sponsored hacker whose job is to incapacitate an "enemy's" digital infrastructure. Since so much of our existence is tied up with computers and computer-controlled processes and because we are so thoroughly interconnected, just the wrong pandemic of computer viruses could tangle up big parts of our lives.

- **Solar flare:** The surface of the sun is quite active and frequently has large "energy releases" with coronal mass ejections. Some years they are more frequent than others, and when the flare/ejection is pointed at the earth, the particles and energy can reach the earth as quickly as fifteen minutes or as long as a couple of days later, causing a geomagnetic storm. In 1989, a large geomagnetic storm struck the earth and knocked a Canadian power system offline for nine hours. It interfered with shortwave radio transmissions and temporarily disabled a weather satellite. A bigger event than this might have even more impact.

Because computers are entangled in so many parts of our lives, it is difficult to predict possible effects, but we might see disruption of the following:

- **Banks/financial services:** Electronic transfers of funds could be interrupted, ATMs could stop issuing cash, and debt payment records could be fouled up. Keep some paper copies of key records like mortgages, loans, insurance policies, and the payments you make against them. Also, keep some cash on hand to make purchases if electronic cash registers and credit card machines stop functioning for a time.

- **Production and distribution of food and consumer products:** Factories may have production problems, and warehousing/transportation companies may have distribution problems. They may be related to inventory shortages, or they may simply be unable to retrieve and fill orders from balky computers. Store a couple of weeks—a couple of months if you can—of food and essential products (think *toilet paper*). These potential shortages will not last long, but you want the option of not having to fight in store aisles for scarce supplies.

- **Telephones/communication systems:** The communications industry is one of the most technologically advanced and, therefore, one of the most vulnerable to technological disruptions. For example, if a satellite were to malfunction, millions could be without phones, data, news, or weather observation. On the plus side, the communications industry also has one of the fastest turnovers for equipment and employs some of the best technical talent to enable it to quickly fix itself.

- **Utilities** (including water, power, natural gas, and sewage systems): Water purification and distribution, power distribution, and sewage processing plants all have electronic control systems, software, and embedded chips and, therefore, some exposure. Could a small failure somewhere cascade into the entire system? The best preparation here is to store some water and prepare for a long-term power outage—have some backup plans for key needs.

- **Personal convenience**: Because of the prevalence of embedded and interconnected computer chips in just about everything, there might be further disruption to elevators, temperature controllers, ventilation systems, security systems, entertainment systems, watches, microwaves, ovens, and cars.

How Do You Prepare?

One of the problems of trying to prepare for a technological emergency is the uncertainty of how widely it could affect an area and how it could affect you personally. Some people will feel no effect, some will have mild effects, and some could have severe effects temporarily. This implies that preparing for technological emergencies should be like preparing for any other possible emergency, such as a severe winter storm. Here are things you could do—and should do—anyway:

- Stay informed, stay current, and agitate for community readiness as well as family readiness.

- Update your readiness. Pull out your 72-hour kit and replace batteries, outdated food, any water that's not sealed, and clothes that children have outgrown. Take inventory and upgrade the items that aren't as functional as you want. Make sure that your water supply stays fresh, and take a look at the food you have stored. Rotate items that are close to expiring and replace them with fresh. How many days or weeks could you go without a trip to the grocery store? If you decide to buy more bulk food items, remember to only buy what your family normally eats anyway. Then replace it as you use it up. Don't forget to make sure you have an up-to-date supply of important drugs and other critical medical supplies.

- Have some cash on hand since an earthquake is just as likely to shake up banks, ATMs, and stores as a technological event is. How much you store is a matter of preference. The more you have, the more you could lose to thieves. Some experts recommend from one to four weeks of cash. If you do decide to increase your cash on hand, do so a little at a time all through the year rather than waiting to do it all at once.

- Plan for an alternate source of heat if you live in a colder climate, like you've intended to do anyway. A power outage in the winter—from any source—can become a matter of safety. Also, extended power outages without alternate heating could result in frozen or burst pipes with additional inconvenience or damage.

- Organize your own computer, clean up the files, and make a backup copy of important files on a separate device, like an external hard drive.

- Organize your financial records and keep recent paper copies around. Mortgages, deeds, loans, payment schedules, insurance of all kinds—maybe in a three-ring binder?

- Don't go buy a cabin in the woods (unless you were going to anyway), don't buy an arsenal, don't convert all of your money to gold bars, and don't sever all ties with civilization just yet. Prepare for technology emergencies just like you would any other potential emergency.

Emergency preparedness:
Do one thing today.

SOCIAL UNREST

When a Crowd Gets out of Control

January 2013, Detroit: About three thousand people waiting in a cold line to get rent assistance vouchers rushed the doors of a first-come-first-served event that didn't have enough vouchers for everyone. Harried officials panicked and turned out the lights and tried to close. The crowd erupted and stormed the facility; fights broke out, and local police had to retreat until state police could arrive.

July 2012, Anaheim: Two police-involved shootings were being protested by a largely peaceful crowd of about five hundred. Then someone in the crowd pelted police with rocks. When police fought back, the crowd turned ugly. The protests lasted over four days, with a Molotov cocktail thrown, windows smashed, looting, injuries, and arrests. Many compared the unrest to the riots of April 1992, when a Los Angeles jury verdict in the Rodney King case was the catalyst for six days of rioting, arson, looting, violence, and murder. In the 1992 riot, curfews were instituted and National Guard troops were deployed before things got under control. When it was over, more than fifty people were dead, over two thousand were injured, and around a billion dollars in damage was done, much of it in neighborhoods least able to bear it. Thousands of businesses were torched, looted, or destroyed. It was worse than the five-day riot in Watts in 1965 (thirty-four dead) and the racial riots in Detroit in 1967 (forty-three dead).

February 2012, Egypt: Thousands of soccer fans stormed the field to celebrate an upset victory in Port Said, Egypt. Police fired tear gas, and fans stampeded the exits only to find several locked and chained. Seventy-nine people died in the riot, sparking additional riots around the country. Soccer (and other sports) riots are reported frequently every year.

Riots occur frequently in our society. They occur when a great injustice is perceived to have occurred. They occur on college campuses, usually accompanied by great quantities of beer. They occur when strikers demonstrate. Or when police try to control demonstrators, like the Occupy Wall Street protesters. They occur at sporting events, sometimes because of a loss, sometimes because of a win. They occur in small cities as well as large urban areas.

Riots are similar to other types of emergencies—there is little or no warning, although in some instances, signs of escalation are apparent. There is no way to know how severe or long lasting they will be. They impact different neighborhoods in different ways, confounding a one-size-fits-all response: in some cases staying put is best; in some cases evacuation is best. In all cases, a little preparation and forethought can affect your outcome.

What Is a Riot?

A riot is the coordinated violent and destructive actions of a large number of people. The first ingredient in the mix is a crowd. An event or well-publicized signal—like an assassination or a national/international sports victory—occurs, and crowds spontaneously gather in prominent places without recruitment. In some cases, the crowd is recruited through social media. In order for a riot to start, a significant fraction of the crowd must believe the crowd will become violent. The fact that they stay means they desire it to become violent. If the crowd is big enough, then individuals in the crowd feel immune to arrest or punishment. All it takes after that is a catalyzing event, like a rock through a window, to trigger violence and looting. Another catalyzing event could be a first strike or even a rumored first strike by a policeman, even if he is using crowd control and nonlethal technologies like beanbag bullets or pepper spray. The crowd will act as a mass, typically overwhelming police or even troops. The crowd commits looting, arson, vandalism, even violence. Armed rioters can become deadly. Some opportunists take advantage of the general anarchy to attack icons of long-standing tension. In Los Angeles in 1992, for example, although the jury decision acquitted white police officers of criminal behavior in beating a black man, much of the violence was focused on Korean-run grocery stores. In locations away from the riots, snipers ambushed police officers and fired on firemen responding to emergency calls.

Witnesses and survivors of riots describe fires, looting, beatings, shootings. Vandalism consists of arson, broken windows, overturned cars. When the police are overwhelmed and retreat, the witnesses realize they are alone, and no one can help them. The looting can become so intense that cars of the looters can cause traffic jams in the looted neighborhood. Business owners intent on defending their shops might arm themselves, adding to the possibility of lethal violence. In intense encounters, police fire tear gas and nonlethal—and sometimes lethal—weapons into the riotous crowds. Secondary effects of several days of widespread rioting include runs on banks, long lines at stores, and lines at gas stations. Public services may be temporarily terminated.

Preparing to Survive a Riot

The first rule of riot survival is to stay out of riots. Avoid riot-prone situations. It is not necessary to avoid all public gatherings, although it would seem wise to stay out of large intoxicated crowds. Pay attention to the mood of the crowd. Get out before it gets ugly; you will frequently have warning that things are edging toward violence. This goes for city council meetings as well as World Cup soccer games. If you can't get out, get to the edges where you can use your surroundings to protect you.

You may not be in the riot when it starts, but you may blunder into it, or it may overtake your neighborhood or transportation route. As in any emergency situation, the more you know from reliable sources, the better. Listen to the most reliable news source you can find in tense situations. Ignore unsubstantiated rumors. If violence breaks out, completely avoid the areas where it is reported. Give the riots a wide berth, knowing that action hot spots could spread. Once the violence gets started, it could break out in other places as well, so for the duration of the riots, it would be wise to avoid prominent public places. Sightseeing is completely out, unless you think that the one blurry snapshot you'll get of the riot is worth your life.

Prepare to hunker down in your house or office. This is where it is handy to have 72-hours of self-sufficiency in the form of a kit. You may need to take care of your family's needs—even in the absence of utilities—for several days in order to avoid going out into the streets. If you work in an urban center, you may have to ride out a riot in your office. Prepare a 72-hour kit for your office and keep it at your desk. If it is in your car, you may be exposed if you have to retrieve it. Even if you are away from the reported violence, you may want to avoid the crowds and lines at stores and gas stations anyway. If your family is separated and you cannot communicate directly for any reason, call your out-of-state contact. Check on neighbors, especially the elderly and infirm, if you can do so safely.

Prepare to leave your house if it becomes necessary. If there is a chance that the violence could progress to your area, you should leave immediately. The first step is to know where you are going. There may be public shelters, or you may have family or friends out of the area you can go to. As soon as your decision is made, contact separated members of your family or call your out-of-state contact. Let them know what time you expect to arrive at your destination. Assure that your evacuation path will not take you through the areas of violence. Take your 72-hour kits and the extra things that you have room and time for. Make sure that you have a current inventory of household goods to document any insurance claims you may have to make. Do not load up the car with belongings that would advertise you as a refugee. Take your less mobile neighbors if they will go with you.

What to Do If Caught in a Riot

- If driving, keep moving. Get through the danger areas quickly. Most riots, even widespread ones, have areas of less intense action. You may be able to drive out of a riot area within a few blocks.

- If on foot, try to get to a public building, hospital, or hotel, unless that is the direction the crowd is flowing. If so, move away from the crowd. You may be able to walk away from the most violent areas within a block or two.

- If the riot begins in your neighborhood or surrounds your apartment, residence, or place of work, your best course of action may be to stay put. Only you can decide if you want to try to escape during a lull in the violence. In many riots, a dusk-to-dawn curfew is imposed and enforced by troops.

- Stay out of sight from the street and stay below window level. Stray and not-stray bullets could be a danger.

- Because arson is so common in riots, post a fire watch: someone should stay awake to alert the rest if your building is set on fire.

- Listen to the news on your battery-powered radio if the electricity is off. Believe your own eyes and ears in preference to the news— if the media reports the violence is diminishing but you do not believe it is safe to go out, then stay put.

- Believe the news in preference to rumors you may hear from neighbors. Distortions and fabrications can run rampant during a period of violence.

Other Crowd Scenes

Of course, there are other crowd scenes that can get out of control. Every year there are numerous reports of stampedes in clubs, theaters, and stadiums where people are crushed, suffocated, or trampled. In these cases, your brain is your only tool—don't lose it to panic. When you go into a public place like a theater or a stadium, note where *all* of the exits are. Try to notice how you would be able to find each exit in total darkness. If a stampede develops, try to stay out of it. You'll have better luck if you can stay put until the crowd subsides and then choose an uncrowded exit. If a fire is causing the panic, get close to the ground while waiting for the panic to subside. If you are unavoidably caught up in the rush, try to move to edges but don't try to counter the flow. Your best bet may be to "surf" the flow and concentrate on keeping your feet beneath you.

If you have teenagers attending concerts, advise them to avoid the largely uncontrolled, frequently overcrowded "mosh pit" area in front of the stage. In recent years, several kids have died as nonviolent crowds surged and asphyxiated them.

Many of our favorite experiences are more fun because there is a crowd: athletic events, concerts, movies, clubs. Not many types of crowds are dangerous. But if you find yourself in an unruly crowd, plan now to keep your head; it is your best protection.

Emergency preparedness:
Do one thing today.

TERRORISM

No Special Preparation for Terrorism

Although it has been over a decade since the 9/11 attacks, terrorism is still on our minds and a big part of our lives. And we worry about the possible shape of future attacks. What might someone intent only upon disruption and damage do to us? What if we don't know what it will be? Is there something we should do to prepare for terrorism? Is there anything we can do?

Yes, preparation for terrorism amounts to doing what we know we need to do anyway. In the end, the world has not changed as much as our perception of it. There have always been people who wish to destroy others. There have always been people who hated Americans or our institutions. There have always been terrorists. There have always been vulnerabilities, and perhaps there always will. The difference is we now see what we didn't before. Do we need to drastically overhaul our preparedness to be ready for the different possibilities of terrorism? Probably not. Let's look at the risks.

Transportation Disruption

The airport part of this is easiest to imagine because we live with it. But terrorists could also halt road, rail, and harbor operations with easily imagined acts. Is this a new threat? Not really. We have always been dependent upon others to bring items produced in other locations to us. Natural causes disrupt transportation too, such as earthquakes, severe storms, or flooding. If transport ceased for a period of time, existing local supplies of food and fuel would be consumed quickly. It seems likely, however, that even a major terrorist disruption would only last several days or maybe a week or two. Preparation, then, consists of storing supplies to carry you through two weeks with no grocery store trips. Store what you already eat rather than something completely foreign. List your menu for two weeks and calculate the quantities required. Now buy double of each item, as steadily as your budget allows. Over the course of several shopping trips, you will be able to lay in everything you need.

Power Disruption

Power generation and distribution systems are somewhat vulnerable to terrorism because they are aging and fragile. If plants or transmission systems are damaged in an attack, then we could have rationing or even lose power completely for some time. But is this a new threat? Not really. Many natural causes, such as earthquakes or severe storms—think of Superstorm Sandy—could impact our power at any time. Preparation consists of identifying alternative sources of heat and light, and alternative methods of cooking food. You probably have an outdoor stove of some kind that will provide alternate cooking for several days. If you have a charcoal barbecue, you can store solid fuel as an option. Safety first: don't cook indoors or heat your home with charcoal; it produces toxic carbon monoxide. If candles or kerosene lanterns are your alternate lighting, an adult should oversee every open flame for safety.

Water Supplies Disruption

We don't even need to imagine terrorists; only a few years ago, a dead raccoon contaminated my small suburban city's water system for nearly a week. Could someone intentionally cause disruption? Probably, but once again, preparation consists of doing what you ought to do anyway. Store a gallon of water per person per day for two weeks. A fifty-five-gallon drum will meet the needs of a family of four. For some luxury, like laundry or baths, store more. Water heaters contain forty to fifty gallons. Make sure the drum is new or has only stored food-grade materials; fuel or chemicals could leach into the water. Clean the drum thoroughly before filling and add bleach, eight drops per gallon. Water in spas, pools, and water beds is undrinkable. Replace stored water every six to twelve months.

Illness/Germ Terrorism

Annual flu and virus season shows us every year that we are vulnerable to biological terrorism. Is this a new threat? Not really; anyone who spends time with other people has always been vulnerable to catching a virulent strain of something contagious. Consider that over fifty million people worldwide died from a natural flu epidemic from 1918 to 1920. Should you stockpile antibiotics? I wouldn't recommend it. Antibiotics have a limited shelf life, and self-diagnosis/self-medication is dangerous. Instead, prepare to be self-sufficient for several days or several weeks so you can avoid contact with infected people.

Chemical Terrorism

This threat seems like a bona fide new concern, but it is just like the risk from any hazardous chemical spill. Any incident will be in a limited area for a limited duration. The only difference is that accidents are random and terrorists will target crowds. Preparation is the same: prepare to evacuate from a hazardous area to a safe one. If you are in a crowd, don't panic; the risk from crowd crush is probably higher than the risk of poisoning. If you are in a building or neighborhood that is asked to evacuate, grab your 72-hour kits and follow recommended routes to safety. The communications plan you already have will tell you how to contact other members of your family. Should you get a gas mask? Only you can decide, but consider that gas masks must be sized and fitted to each face, and they must be maintained and tested regularly. As children grow, they will need new masks. You also need to have the right (and functioning) filter cartridge for the chemical. And it must be with you when you need it—are you really going to take it to the big game?

Nuclear Terrorism

For those of us who grew up in the duck-and-cover 1960s, this is not a new threat. In today's environment, we could look at sabotaged nuclear power plants and improvised "dirty bomb" nuclear weapons. But the threat is limited: it may hit somewhere, but it won't hit everywhere. What should our preparation be? By now you can work this out: preparation for natural disasters will give the most options in a nuclear scenario.

Product Tampering

A few well-publicized cases of product tampering could undermine our confidence in products at the grocery store, denying access to food and supplies. But product tampering has been around much longer than even organized terrorists and is something we must be aware of anyway. In addition to being cautious consumers and paying attention to recalls and warnings, we can store some extra food that will see us safely through a supply crisis. Once again, the things we do to prepare for other emergencies will serve us here as well.

Economic Impact

In the long term, it seems that widespread economic downturn will be the most likely and the most impactful result of terrorism. Unemployment may rise and production may decline. But we know what to do here too because as individuals we have always had the risk of layoffs or serious illness or accident: live frugally, within your income; stay out of debt; put aside emergency funds; store some food and supplies.

• • •

The chances of terrorism directly impacting us are small, maybe even smaller than the threat of earthquake or tornado; the chances we could be impacted by the larger reaction to a distant terrorist attack are much higher. But we don't need to do more or do different things; we only need to do what we know to do anyway.

Emergency preparedness: Do one thing today (that you should be doing anyway).

FINANCIAL EMERGENCIES

Preparing for Financial Disasters

Sometimes it is easy to take our personal and national economic systems for granted: how much we get paid, where our money is kept, how we can trade it for goods and services, how much things cost. But given the fragility of our personal financial lives, it makes sense to evaluate the kinds of financial disasters that could impact us and look at the measures we might take to mitigate them.

Personal Financial Disaster

This type of disaster can come about for a variety of reasons: perhaps you were "downsized" out of your job or an injury or illness caused the family's primary wage earner to miss work. Think about it: how many paychecks in a row could you afford to miss? A legal judgment against you or high medical bills not covered by insurance could also cause personal financial crisis, as could the failure of the bank or savings institution that stores your money. To mitigate the effects of any of these occurrences, consider the following:

- Maintain appropriate insurance. A primary wage earner with dependents should have several types of insurance: homeowner's or renter's (make sure the policy is for replacement value of home and possessions, and make sure you have some liability coverage), auto insurance, life insurance (an agent will help you calculate the amount necessary), health insurance (at least some sort of a "catastrophic" coverage), and disability insurance. In all cases, you should seek advice from a trusted insurance agent. In most cases, insurance is not intended as a ladder to higher prosperity but as a safety net to prevent complete financial destitution.

- Maximize your education. Income studies show that the best paying, most stable jobs in our society are held by those best educated. More education typically means more money and more stability. Take advantage of every educational opportunity at your disposal. If you were not able to finish that college degree years ago, start back now with night classes or home-study or online courses. If you have the skills but not the classwork to nail down that certificate or license, there is no better time than the present. Community colleges, trade schools, and universities all have programs to accommodate the working person, and many companies offer tuition reimbursement to reduce your out-of-pocket costs. Also take advantage of every course offered by your employer. These continuing education courses are usually free or at a greatly reduced cost and will enhance your current skills or expose you to other new and interesting areas. Read books and periodicals both in your field and in related or even totally new ones.

- Be employable. In your current job, be on time, dependable, honest, hardworking, pleasant, and creative. Try to improve the breadth and depth of your own skills. Also try to understand your job in the larger context of the overall company. Try to learn about jobs of the others around you. Those who are flexible and versatile and easy to work with are usually not the first ones laid off.

- Get out of debt and stay out of debt. There are a number of good programs available to assist you if your debt is out of control. Stop charging anything you cannot pay off on the next credit card statement. Cut up all of your credit cards except one for emergencies. Be careful about refinancing consumer debt into your house mortgage. Pay close attention to the terms of any loans and be especially wary of home equity loans that can put your house at risk.

- Practice saving. Pay yourself the first 10 percent of every paycheck. After you have saved up a month or two of living expenses—in an account separate from your household account and maybe in a different institution—put this money into a long-term savings account; don't use it to finance the boat upgrade or the extravagant vacation. The more you invest early in your life, the sooner you can assure your financial independence. If your company has a 401K program with matching contributions, get into it as soon as possible and contribute enough to get the maximum match.

- Develop other marketable skills. Explore other skills you might be interested in: real estate, investing, electronics, computers, writing, sewing, crafts. Explore them as hobbies at first, but try to determine if there is any moneymaking potential in them. Who is making money in these fields? How are they doing it? Are there any certifications that you need? Any special equipment? How could you use this skill if you needed to fall back on it? Don't neglect the talents/skills of both spouses. While one spouse can be a primary wage earner, the other could be going to school to enhance earning potential. A part-time job could keep less employed spouses current in their skills, even if they spend most of their time as the primary caregiver of children.

- Put away some food storage. Pick a cool, dry location in your house and build some sturdy shelves. Then watch for sales of items your family eats anyway and buy in bulk. You can put away food gradually that will last you for weeks or months, which might be all you need to tide you over during an unexpected job change or financial hardship. Mark each food storage item with the date of purchase so you can rotate it to prevent spoilage.

- Spread your savings around. Try to keep your emergency liquid account—a month or two of living expenses—in a different bank or savings and loan than your primary household account. This will prevent troubles in a single financial institution from completely devastating your family.

- Practice frugality. Remember the old rhyme: Use it up, wear it out, make it do, or do without. Learn how to maintain and repair your home and items in your home. Learning these skills will not only enable you to live more frugally but may also be marketable skills themselves in a financial crisis. Resist the urge to buy more *stuff* just because it is there. Simplify your life and get by with less. Do you really need all of the clothes in your closet now? Or all of the personal grooming chemistry? Or all of the mechanical or electronic toys and gadgets? Every new thing you buy is something else that will require time and maintenance, further complicating your life. Simplify.

Financial Complications following Another Emergency

An earthquake, extensive flooding, severe storm pattern, or even social unrest could make money inaccessible from banks and ATMs for some period. Here are some things you can do in advance:

- Store some cash in your 72-hour kits. While it is not wise to store large amounts of cash, several hundred dollars in small bills (store some coins too) will give you some flexibility in any purchases you need to make before the area's financial resources are restored.

- Food storage (see previous page) is useful in any emergency. Consider storing some goods you could use to trade and barter. In a short-term emergency, seemingly common items like toilet paper, candles, matches, charcoal, or drink flavoring might be in demand. Convenience foods like meal-in-a-can items might also be useful for barter.

- Don't go it alone. Check on your neighbors and pool resources. Others may have what you lack.

Global Financial Turmoil

A global financial crisis, while a remote possibility, could develop if the right (or wrong) conditions were present. Global inflation or depression could develop, literally changing all of the rules. In this sort of situation, no amount of preparation will ready you for all of the conditions that could arise, but the following could help.

- Put away some food storage.

- Depending on the nature of the crisis, money may or may not have value. In some circumstances, for example, hyperinflation renders legal tender useless. Some observers recommend putting some emergency funds away in gold or silver. This has its advantages like giving you some stable purchasing power under a variety of conditions. It also has some disadvantages, chief of which is the vulnerability to theft. Additionally, gold and silver may not be very negotiable, and it would be difficult to store small enough denominations to be useful. Be aware that homeowner's insurance policies do not cover theft of any significant amount of cash.

- If the crisis is deep and widespread, then your first priority is to provide the basics for your family: shelter, food, water, medical care, sanitation. Whatever society does not or cannot provide, you must create yourself. But don't go it alone. Team up with your neighbors and neighborhood to create a community. Pool your skills, your resources, and your energy. A group is more likely to thrive under difficult circumstances than a single family. In a long-term, widespread financial emergency, a trade-and-barter economy may develop. Consider storing some goods that store well and could be in demand—soap/shampoo, detergent, spices, candles, sanitation supplies. Skills are also useful commodities to trade. If you have some valuable skills, make sure you have supplies on hand to enable you to "ply your trade" in an emergency.

• • •

Financial crises can strike us without warning, whether they are individual or global in nature. Take some steps now to reduce their impact on your family's lives.

Insurance: An Important Part of Financial Emergency Preparedness

Buying insurance is a classic example of preparing for an emergency. In the case of homeowner's or property insurance, you are assuring your financial recovery from many kinds of disasters. Here are a few insurance tips from a veteran claims adjuster and insurance agent:

1. Know what your policy covers and what its limits are. Excavate your policy from that pile of papers and read it. You'll probably understand a lot more of it than you think. Your insurance agent can help if you have questions; he or she wants you to know your policy too. Don't hesitate to request an insurance review with your agent whenever you feel like your coverage may not be adequate. When you are done reading it, make a copy to keep and put your policy in a safe place with other important papers. You'll want to make sure you know exactly where it is in an emergency.

Most homeowners have a type of insurance called a "special form" policy. This type usually covers a wide variety of disasters (high winds, winter storms, vandalism, theft, fire, and so on) except those explicitly excluded. Common exclusions are earthquake and flooding. The special form policy also usually guarantees replacement of the structure, which means that inflation is accounted for.

If you have a policy with a replacement value specified ("face value"), you'll need to upgrade every few years to make sure you could rebuild your home if required. If you have any question about your type of insurance or its coverage and limits, read your policy; it's all in there.

2. Evaluate your deductible level. The deductible is the amount you would have to pay following a disaster before your insurance coverage takes over. The deductible will be stated in your policy. You could consider increasing the deductible to lower the premium.

3. Add earthquake and flood insurance to your policy. Again, a standard homeowner's policy does *not* cover earthquakes. Earthquake "endorsements" are additions to your policy to reimburse you for earthquake damage. Remember that earthquake endorsements have a separate deductible (typically five to ten percent of the face value) and have a maximum reimbursement limit specified. This means that if you have a one hundred thousand dollars face value and a five percent deductible, the insurance company will reimburse you ninety-five thousand after you pay the first five thousand. You should review the face value of an earthquake endorsement every few years to make sure that your coverage will enable you to replace your home if necessary. Common claims after an earthquake relate to cracking of walls and ceilings, and collapsing chimneys. This kind of damage can be expensive to repair.

Homeowner's policies usually cover flooding from internal sources, such as broken pipes, leaky fixtures, and so on. A standard homeowner's policy typically does not cover flooding when the water comes from outside of the house. When you see your agent about flood coverage, he or she will consult a FEMA flood map to determine the risk zone your home is in. This is a standard flood map prepared by the government and defines drainage and groundwater risks. The cost of your flood insurance will depend upon the flood risks to which you are exposed. Be aware that you can also buy a "disaster policy" that covers both earthquake and flood, often at a competitive price. Ask your agent.

4. Review your business insurance needs. If you own a business, you may have unique insurance needs, depending on the type and size of business. You may need property insurance and liability insurance. You may need professional liability or "errors and omissions" insurance. You should review your specialized business insurance needs with your agent.

• • •

Even though insurance can't prevent a disaster, it can give you the peace of mind that you can get back on your feet quickly following an emergency. In fact, after a disaster, insurance companies send out extra claims adjusters to the disaster area for prompt processing and payout of claims so clients can rebuild immediately. Your objective should be to make sure that your insurance coverage matches your needs.

Emergency preparedness:
Do one thing today.

PART 3

EMERGENCY PREPAREDNESS AS A WAY OF LIFE

GET STARTED:
10 EASY THINGS TO DO

So maybe you have read straight through this book. Or maybe you have flipped around and looked at things that are interesting. Or maybe you have come back to it after some major event in the world—or your neighborhood—has jolted you. In any of these cases, you may still be scratching your head saying, "Where do I start?" Here are ten ideas for starting. If you want to get started simply, do the basic list. If you have more ambition (plus time, money, and energy), move to the deluxe list.

1. Family Plan

- **Basic**: Make an emergency contact plan. Identify a friend or relative outside of the immediate area (preferably outside the state) that everyone in the family can call to relay messages. In an emergency, it may be easier to make long-distance calls than local ones. Put important phone numbers on a card for everyone in the family.

- **Deluxe**: Add a get-together plan. Where do you spend your time? Work, school, friends' houses? Discuss how you will get from each location to your home in an emergency and the routes you will take. Select a primary reunion location, like your home; then select a secondary reunion location out of the immediate area, in case you are not able to get home. Don't forget to consider the emergency plans and policies that schools have in place.

2. The No-Kidding Emergency Flashlight

- **Basic**: Buy a good, solid flashlight with a wide and bright beam.

Buy extra batteries and bulbs. Declare this as the no-kidding emergency light. Threaten severe consequences to anyone who even thinks about using it for some other project or game. Put it in an easy-to-get-to, easy-to-find location that you can find by touch.

- **Deluxe:** Buy some extra inexpensive flashlights and a battery lantern. Have a lights-out practice one evening where you turn off all of the lights and don't do anything that requires electricity. Have a reading night or a board game night. You may have to plan ahead for electricity-less snacks.

3. Utilities

- **Basic:** Find out where the gas, water, and electricity shutoffs are.
- **Deluxe:** Teach everyone in your family where the shutoffs are and when/how to turn them off. Put the proper tools in a known place.

4. Fire Safety

- **Basic:** Identify two escape routes out of every room. Pick a spot outside your home to get back together. Have a family council and talk about getting out of the house, and how to stop, drop, and roll.
- **Deluxe:** Walk through your house with a paper and pen and look for fire safety problems: overloaded sockets; worn wires; clutter near the furnace or water heater; expired fire extinguishers; fire hazards around space heaters, fireplaces, and stoves; battery-less or broken smoke detectors or carbon monoxide detectors. Then fix things that need to be fixed.

5. 72-Hour Kits

- **Basic:** Get a large box or a plastic tote and get the list on page 24—spend fifteen minutes collecting as many things on the list as you already have hanging around the house. You'll be surprised at how much you already have.
- **Deluxe:** Make a shopping list of all of the things you don't have and go get them. Finish the kit and put it—in a portable container or duffle—in an easy place to find if you need to grab it and go with no warning.

6. Water

- **Basic:** Store a couple gallons per person (72-hour supply) in two-liter plastic soda bottles.

- **Deluxe:** Calculate how much water you need if everyone in the family gets a gallon a day for two weeks. Find the right bulk container and get that water stored.

7. Food

- **Basic:** Buy extra groceries, enough to make three to five of your regular meals. Store these meals.

- **Deluxe:** Actually make a list and a plan to acquire supplies for a couple of week's—or even a month's—meals.

8. First Aid

- **Basic:** Collect all of the first-aid supplies you have in your house right now into a box or a bin. Compare it to the list on pages 39–40. Go shopping.

- **Deluxe:** Get online, call your local fire department, or ask your supervisor at work and find a first-aid and CPR class and get signed up.

9. Neighbor Networks

- **Basic:** Pick one neighbor to be your "preparedness buddy." This is someone who will check on you, and you will check on them, in an emergency. Have that first discussion. You may find it motivational to have someone else to work with.

- **Deluxe:** Look into CERT (community emergency response team) classes and organize your whole block to work together in an emergency.

10. Information

- **Basic:** Gather all of the information you've been collecting—articles, books, and clippings—into one place.

- **Deluxe:** Organize your files by topic and put them in a three-ring binder. You may actually have to read some of them.

• • •

The most important thing to remember if you are just starting out is to do one thing today. And then do another thing tomorrow.

Emergency preparedness:
Do one thing today.

LIFE PREPAREDNESS: SHARING INFORMATION

It happens. Sometimes it's natural and expected. Sometimes it's sudden and tragic. It's always disruptive. Within hours of the death of someone you depend on, you will have to answer important questions and make decisions. In the days and weeks following their passing, you will be required to shoulder their responsibilities: child care, house and car maintenance, bills, taxes. Imagine how difficult it would be if your spouse died. Now imagine how difficult it would be for your spouse if you died. Getting your life in order now could spare your loved ones unpleasant surprises and the burden of trying to organize a mess after you are gone. Here are some principles to use in organizing your life:

Gather Information into a Single Location

Gather all you can find now. Every time you find a new piece of information, put it with the rest. Use a three ring binder and pocket dividers to organize the papers, including:

- Deeds to real estate, titles to automobiles or other property
- Mortgages, loan agreements
- Insurance policies
- Investment papers and reports
- Retirement and pension plan information
- Savings and bank accounts
- Medical history, records, consent forms

161

- Important certificates: birth, death, marriage

- Military papers

- Divorce papers or records of other legal proceedings

- Income tax records

- Wills, living wills, advanced medical directives, organ donor papers

Protect Important Papers

Make copies of important, irreplaceable papers and put originals in a fireproof, theft-proof location. Some people buy a safe for their home. Others are better off renting a safe-deposit box at a bank. You and your spouse both need to know which bank the box is in and where the key is. It's a good idea to inform a third person, in case something happens to both of you at the same time.

Share Financial Information

Both you and your spouse should understand the regular and the long-term finances, including budget, debts/loans, and monthly bills. Keep a complete list of bank and investment accounts, and make sure that more than one can sign on each of them. Keep a list of credit cards (also handy if you lose your wallet or purse). Check deeds and mortgages; ownership should be in both names ("joint tenants"), or you'll need to otherwise ensure that death will not make assets unavailable to the survivor. You both should know the terms and conditions of all loans and mortgages. Make sure that you both understand what retirement benefits you are entitled to and whom to contact.

Make Sure You Are Protected

Consult an insurance agent about the type and amount of life insurance you have. Insurance needs evolve as obligations come and go. Make sure your beneficiary information is up-to-date, especially if you are married. Keep all records together. Seek competent legal advice about creating a simple will. It needn't be complicated nor expensive; your goal is to ensure that your family is not legally or financially stranded if you die. Record your desires for the distribution of personal effects as a part of the will or make a separate list. Write it all down; no one can remember that much.

It is also important to dictate the medical care you wish to receive if you cannot make your own decisions. Some people want no heroic (and expensive) or artificial measures taken if they have no reasonable chance of recovery. You should seek legal advice if you want to create a binding document. If you want to be an organ donor, make sure you have the correct paperwork and tell your family members; they will be the ones asked to sign the donor forms at a critical emotional time.

Learn Each Other's Jobs

After years of living together, most couples fall into comfortable roles. One may take care of the finances and household while the other takes care of house, yard, and car maintenance. If your spouse passed away, would you know how to do what he or she does? Trade household roles for a month or six. Learn what your spouse does and then help him or her learn your jobs. Besides learning how to keep the household running, you also get to spend time together and get a fresh perspective on your relationship. After the trade, you won't take your spouse for granted again.

Or try this exercise: write the instructions that you would give to a babysitter/house sitter if you were going on a two-week vacation. (It would even be more fun if you then took the two-week vacation.) Don't forget kids' schedules, household routines, pets, alarms, and so on. You get the picture. You may already have done something like this. Decide if the instructions change depending on the season. Now add instructions you might give to someone who will live in your house while the whole family tours Europe (or choose your fantasy) for six months. Include things like winterizing the house, the sprinkler system, and the RVs; water and electricity shutoff; yard maintenance; and car upkeep. Does your house or car have little quirks that might alarm or confuse someone new to them? Include your tricks. Don't worry about capturing every detail of your life—you'll know when it's enough. The question to ask is: could my spouse do this if I were gone?

Make Plans Now

Whom do you want (or need) to be notified when you die? What aspects of your life would you want in your obituary? (Be frugal with the words—long obits can be expensive.) Where would you like to be buried? Do you own a burial plot? Where, exactly? Do you want cremation? Who should speak (or not speak) at your funeral? Do you want flowers or contributions to a charity? If you have wishes, write them down (memory fades) and give them to the people who will be responsible for making decisions when you are gone. But be considerate; your loved ones may find comfort in fulfilling your wishes, but they may also suffer guilt if you give instructions that are impractical.

List the Experts in Your Lives

Doctor, dentist, orthodontist, mechanic, plumber, furnace repairman, lawyer, accountant, pharmacist, lawn care expert, alarm company, stock broker, insurance agent, banker, and so on—these people know your situation and are in the best position to help you keep your life together.

Businesses Require Special Attention

If you own a business or income properties, you have more information to gather. What are the debts? What contracts do you have? Who is dependent upon the business? Could it function without you? Who best knows how to run it? Who could liquidate the business most effectively? If you want your business to survive you, it might be worth your while to invest either time or money in a detailed contingency plan.

• • •

"Putting your life in order" is a gift to your loved ones. Putting your life in order doesn't mean that trouble will come any sooner. It doesn't mean that trouble will be prevented. It does, however, mean that your family will have less confusion and worry should the unexpected happen. And that is what emergency preparedness is all about.

Emergency preparedness:
Do one thing today.

NEIGHBORS HELP
EACH OTHER

In the 1944 Alfred Hitchcock movie *Lifeboat*, survivors of a torpedoed boat are thrown together and must make the best of the situation. In an emergency, we could find ourselves in a similar situation with the people in our neighborhood. Imagine a large earthquake, for example. Utilities are damaged, communications are out, roads are damaged, and supplies cannot get into the area. Movement within the damaged zone is severely restricted. Emergency services are overwhelmed—everyone is on their own. Or are they? In emergency preparedness, we strive for self-sufficiency, yet that ignores a vital part of the equation: none of us is truly alone if we live in a neighborhood. As individuals, we are vulnerable to almost everything, yet there is almost nothing that a neighborhood can't face together. Why? Because each of us has different resources and skills to contribute.

What is a neighborhood? Although we may define it geographically—everyone within certain boundaries—a neighborhood is best defined as a collection of like-minded people who know and help each other. Do the people have to be demographically homogeneous for a neighborhood to work? No. All ages, races, sexes, religions, and economic classes have something to offer each other in times of emergency. Some may have medical skills, some may have construction skills, and some may have communications skills. Others may contribute supplies or equipment. But when these people put their best effort together in a common cause, no emergency situation is too daunting.

Creating a Cooperative Neighborhood

So how do you create a neighborhood that helps each other? Neighborhood cooperation begins with neighbors knowing neighbors, and it has to be rooted in understanding and respect. This process can start small: get to know your next-door neighbors. Go introduce yourself and your family. If you are embarrassed, take over a plate of cookies as an excuse. Or plan your introduction to coincide with a holiday or a celebration so it seems less forced. Once you do it, you'll find that it's not as hard as you think. It takes time to get to know someone, so plan on spending some time doing things with them: go to dinner or a community event, or have a barbecue in your yard. Get to know their children's names.

Once you know a few neighbors, getting to know others is easier. Get to know the parents of your children's friends—you probably have a lot in common with them. Is there someone who is the social ringleader of the area? Get to know them, and you'll have ready-made introductions to your other neighbors. Walk around your neighborhood when the weather is good. Wave to people when you see them. Stop and introduce yourself to people in their yards. If there is any kind of block party or neighborhood gathering, go to it. Be a little outgoing as you try to get to know others. It takes effort to establish an open and friendly atmosphere.

If you are the long-term residents, be inclusive of the new family. Meet them when they move in and invite them to neighborhood gatherings. Help them feel part of the group. As you get to know your neighbors, you'll be in a better position to identify others who may be receptive to working together on neighborhood projects like emergency preparedness or neighborhood watch programs.

What Organized Neighborhoods Can Do

A neighborhood that acts together can be a powerful force:

- Neighbors can look after each other on a day-to-day basis. Neighbors with special needs such as health problems or reduced mobility can receive help from those who live close to them. My own father was first to any neighbor's aid; later when he had to be in a wheelchair, a neighbor often came to help out when my father took a tumble. Neighbors can assist each other on a day-to-day basis and can make sure that the special needs are met even in an emergency.

Who can respond faster or with better understanding than a neighbor who knows his neighbor's needs?

- Neighborhoods can form neighborhood watch programs in conjunction with their local police or sheriff's department. Although each law enforcement jurisdiction has its own program, they have many similarities: they raise citizen awareness of burglaries, vandalism, and other crimes in the neighborhood through an information program; they instruct and assist neighborhoods in better property protection through property marking and home security instruction; and they foster neighborhood action programs where neighbors watch each other's property and record and report suspicious activities. Although law enforcement departments can provide the information and the training, the basic organization has to be set up by the neighborhood. One metropolitan neighborhood banded together to get rid of people that were selling drugs from a nearby residence. The neighborhood set up a surveillance of the excessive and odd-hour traffic and presented local authorities with a database listing all of the cars, license plate numbers, descriptions of visitors, and details of odd goings-on. With eyewitnesses and complete and organized information, authorities were able to conduct arrests that shut down the dealers and removed users from the neighborhood.

- Neighborhoods can organize for emergency preparation and response. Some neighborhoods band together to purchase bulk supplies at discount and to distribute preparedness information. Some neighborhoods organize into blocks and create plans so neighbors will check on and assist each other in an emergency.

- Sometimes it takes an emergency to get neighbors together. In a local contaminated-water incident, it was discovered that the best way to disseminate accurate information was by neighbors going door-to-door. And in any kind of evacuation situation, what better, faster, more complete way to notify people than neighbors going door-to-door? In an organized neighborhood, no one would be left out; neighbors know where basement or garage apartments are, and neighbors know who is home and who needs extra help.

- Neighborhoods can be social units with regular social functions like barbecues or block parties or even family outings to recreational areas.

- Neighborhoods can organize as political units. Often the political actions carried out have to do with local issues such as planning and zoning or neighborhood safety.

It Takes a Leader

The clear message is that people can create the kinds of neighborhoods they want to live in. But be aware: if you think that any of this is a good idea, you may have to be the leader—many people will contribute to a good idea, but often it takes a single individual with a vision and some gumption to get it started and keep it rolling. If you wait for someone else to pick up your broad hints, you might have a long wait. Being a neighborhood leader will take up some of your time, but you could consider it an investment in making your corner of the world a nicer place to live. Who wouldn't want to live in a place where people knew, cared about, and supported each other? You can live in such a place, but it may be up to you to get the ball rolling. Like other aspects of emergency preparedness, you have to take some personal responsibility to make it happen.

Emergency preparedness: Meet one neighbor today.

SHARE EMERGENCY PREPARATION INFORMATION IN A FAIR

An important part of emergency preparedness is gathering and sharing information with neighbors and friends. It motivates you and them, and opens doors to creating that caring neighborhood. One way to share information is through a preparedness fair. Anyone—church groups, civic organizations, clubs, Scouts, or even a neighborhood group—can organize a preparedness fair or workshop. For example, a local church group held an emergency preparedness fair. Leaders and members of the group gathered many available resources into a single, information-packed morning. Here are a few lessons they learned.

Pick a Date and a Location

Give yourself four to six weeks to pull everything together. "We made the decision to have the fair about four weeks in advance, but some of our people would have liked more time," said the fair director. The location determines how many and what type of topics you can cover. You may want a single large room for displays, or several smaller rooms for workshops. Some outdoor space gives you flexibility to have cooking demonstrations. This church group had about twenty exhibits in their building and occupied the main hall, the back parking lot, and three or four other rooms. If you don't have a large hall, consider a smaller, single-topic fair. Or if you are a neighbor group, try a "progressive fair" and move from home to home for each topic.

Divide and Conquer

Everyone is an expert at something, or can learn to be. Let individuals or groups (like Scouts or youth groups) create a display on their area of expertise. You'll be surprised at what comes out. Or simply assign topics and watch everyone become experts in their areas.

Use Available Resources

Here is a list of some of the organizations this group utilized in their fair. Most have free information and brochures they are happy to have you distribute. Some will lend you hardware to display or videos to show. Although the organizations listed here are specific to a locale with both rural and metropolitan areas, other locations should have similar resources. Call the public relations department and start asking questions.

- The gas company has brochures on gas safety in general and earthquake preparedness specifically. One favorite is the "scratch and sniff" card to teach kids the smell of gas. They have a model gas meter so people can practice turning off a real gas valve. They also have a small model of a water heater so you can show how to restrain it against tipping.

- The power company can provide brochures and videos on electrical safety for both kids and adults. One of their pamphlets tells what to do in a power outage.

- State departments of environmental health and public health can provide information about water purification and safe drinking water.

- Since the Red Cross mission includes community education, they publish many free pamphlets on family emergency preparation. They can also schedule classes (first aid, CPR, and such) for your group, although some of these may require a fee.

- FEMA has many topics they might be able to help with, either through handouts and brochures, or even direct participation.

- The local fire department is active in community education and cooperative about helping you distribute fire safety and first-aid information. If you schedule far enough in advance, the local station may even be able to send someone to help you demonstrate some of these concepts. They have information on fire safety, fire extinguishers, tips for older folks, and coloring books for kids.

- Local extension services may help disseminate information about gardening, food preparation, and preservation. Printed materials may have a nominal cost.

- The local police or sheriff's department can provide information on child safety, phone safety, latchkey kids, child identification programs, street safety, stranger danger, and so on. They have pamphlets to distribute and videos to loan.

- There are a number of local commercial vendors of emergency preparation supplies. These people usually have lots of good information, but they also have products they are trying to sell. Only you can decide if you want the commercial flavor in your fair.

Focus on Your Group's Own Special Needs

The church group had a number of displays wholly prepared and staffed by their own members and tailored to their own needs. Their "personalized" displays included information on 72-hour kits, cooking in an emergency, car kits, family disaster plans, long-term food storage, protection of valuable papers, and emotional/spiritual preparation. Other ways to focus on your group's needs include inviting an expert to speak about a specific topic, organizing your fair around a theme, presenting mini-classes, and so on.

Don't Forget Follow-Up Activities

If you have enough interest expressed by the group, follow up by scheduling Red Cross CPR and first-aid training courses. Have a local enthusiast schedule a HAM radio class to certify more people in your area. If you have twenty-five to thirty people interested, you can even schedule a CERT (community emergency response team) class with the fire department. In seven sessions you will learn disaster preparedness, fire suppression techniques, first aid, light search and rescue, and team organization/psychology. The class is intended to teach citizens basic skills to respond to emergencies before authorities arrive, and it ends with a disaster simulation.

Whatever your approach, a preparedness fair has many benefits. "Our objective was to educate as many people as possible in emergency preparedness skills," said the fair director. "Those who participated certainly learned a lot." Learning the information, however, is only a first step. The most important thing is to put it into practice.

Emergency preparedness:
Do one thing today.

NETWORKING AND THE
EXPERTS IN YOUR LIVES

Recently, my friend had trouble with the heating system in her new house. She repeatedly took hours off work to meet with electricians, plumbers, and repairmen, each of whom used different diagnostic tools and gave her different answers. After the last round of confusing advice, she said in frustration, "I wish I lived in a neighborhood!"

What she meant was that she wished she had a network of friends and neighbors to whom she could turn for help and advice, people that she trusted, people who had skills and knowledge. In fact, all of us need just such a network, day in and day out. Whether it is a personal emergency like house flooding or heating system breakdown, or whether it is widespread like an earthquake or severe storm, none of us need face it alone. Here are some suggestions for building a network to help out in emergencies:

1. Be Part of Your Neighborhood.

Get to know your next-door neighbors. Introduce yourself. Walk around your neighborhood and wave to people. Stop and talk to people in their yards. If there is a block party or neighborhood gathering, go to it. Be a little outgoing.

2. Network in All of Your Circles

No matter who you are, you participate in a variety of groups ready-made for networking: social circles, work groups, clubs, organizations, church. Actively participate in each of these groups. Be genuinely interested in others, in their lives, families, skills, and problem-solving network. When you have a problem—like trying to find a reliable furnace repairman—ask opinions. Others may have had the same situation and developed trusted contacts.

3. Help and Be Helped

In your network, sometimes it is your turn to help and sometimes it is your turn to be helped. Accept both roles graciously. When it is your turn, actively try to help people. Is a neighbor trying to start a car repair business? Steer some of your other friends that direction. Does a friend have the same difficulty with a child that you had? Share the information you collected. Does a coworker need the same house repairs you just made? They might appreciate a recommendation from someone they know.

Don't think that you have to possess specialized knowledge to help. Taking pizza and cold drinks to a moving neighbor can be a huge help. Watching a neighbor's children or pets during a critical time can be sanity-saving for them. And your skill set is always changing, based on work opportunities, service in church, or even hobbies. Offer them unselfishly when a neighbor or friend needs them.

When it is your turn to be helped, swallow hard and allow it. People would rather network with someone who both gives and takes because it feels more like a community where everyone benefits from each other. When others help you, they become more connected to you, more likely to let you help them, and even more likely to help you again. It is definitely a circle, but it is the opposite of vicious.

4. Develop Appropriate Loyalty with Experts

Building a network is often about repeated contacts with the same people. If you find a car repairman that is proficient, friendly, and reasonably priced, make it a point to take your business there. Frequent the same business establishments when they meet your needs. Of course, this does not mean that you should blindly support someone who is dishonest, unpleasant, or high-priced. It only means that you may tolerate minor inconveniences and even mistakes if the service is generally acceptable the rest of the time. Offer compliments when they are deserved and suggestions when you have them. Good businesses desire honest feedback.

5. Thank Those Who Help You

One of the most powerful network tools is the thank-you note. When someone helps you out, no matter how small, be sure to thank them. For some situations, include a gift. This needn't be pricey or elaborate; a plate of cookies or freshly baked bread shows that you recognize that the other person's help came at some sacrifice and that you appreciate it.

• • •

In the end, my friend with the heating problem realized that she did, indeed, have friends and family who could help her sort out the situation; a brother explained the diagnostic devices, and a repairman she had previously identified helped sort out the advice and provide a path. It takes a lifetime to collect family, friends, neighbors, and associates who can help us through life. And whether you're in an emergency or not, this network makes life easier and more rewarding.

Emergency preparedness: Do one thing today.

EMERGENCY PREPARATION FOR BUSINESSES

Do you operate a business? What events would challenge your ability to function? How would a fire or earthquake disrupt operations? In a disaster, you have two main objectives: protect the safety of staff and customers, and protect your ability to stay in business. After 9/11, it is estimated that thousands of businesses in Manhattan closed.

Basic Principles

- In a business, everything starts at the top; if the boss doesn't value the activity, it won't get done. Also, there will be costs that the boss must approve.

- The leader's job is to watch for threats and decide what emergencies you will prepare for.

- Preparedness will be more thorough and effective if you involve your staff. They will buy into the activity and will better understand what is required of them.

Prevent What Can Be Prevented

Make sure that the disaster doesn't originate in your workplace. Start by walking through and identifying hazards. Bring a pad of paper—you will find more hazards than you think. Write them all down so you can prioritize them for fixing.

- For fire safety, note cluttered workspaces and piles of boxes and papers. Check electrical equipment and look for worn cords or overloaded sockets and circuits, or wires that snake under carpets.

Look for portable heaters, coffee machines, and other electrical devices at workstations. If you are required to use hazardous and flammable materials, the OSHA Hazard Communication Program requirements may apply in their storage, labeling, and disposal. If materials are not needed, dispose of them properly. Check out smoke and carbon monoxide alarms. Replace or recharge old fire extinguishers.

- For employee health and safety, note cluttered workspaces and slip, trip, and fall hazards. Pay special attention to break rooms and kitchens. Make sure that employees who work with power tools, knives, or chemicals have proper safety equipment in addition to a controlled workspace and adequate tools and lighting. Although it's beyond the scope of this book, now might also be a good time to do an ergonomic analysis for each process in your business. Like emergency preparedness, employee well-being is an ongoing process that requires continual support and encouragement. And an injured key employee can be a disaster for a business.

- Determine if your office is in any danger from external flooding. If you are in a floodplain, as shown on FEMA maps, seriously consider moving your operation. Note that there can also be flood hazards from malfunctioning irrigation or water-supply systems. And don't overlook the possibility of in-building flooding. Where do water pipes run? What will be affected if they freeze and break or if a sink upstairs runs all night?

- Look for earthquake hazards. Check hanging fixtures and art. Examine tall furniture. Where will bookshelves fall? Will computer equipment fly off the tables? Will falling furniture block exits? There are relatively simple fixes for each of these things.

- Examine the physical security of your office. Do you need to invest in a security system? How would you be affected if you were the victim of theft or vandalism?

After the hazards walk-through, prioritize the hazards, check the budget, and fix the hazards you found.

Mitigate What Cannot Be Prevented

Many businesses are required by OSHA to have a written emergency action plan. The OSHA requirements (from www.osha.gov; search for "emergency action plan") include

- Procedures for reporting a fire or other emergency
- Procedures for emergency evacuation, including type of evacuation and exit route assignments
- Procedures for employees who remain to operate critical plant operations before they evacuate
- Procedures to account for all employees after evacuation
- Procedures to be followed by employees performing rescue or medical duties
- The name or job title of every employee who may be contacted by employees who need more information about the plan or an explanation of their duties under the plan
- Employee alarm system. An employer must have and maintain an employee alarm system. The employee alarm system must use a distinctive signal for each purpose and comply with OSHA requirements
- Training. An employer must designate and train employees to assist in a safe and orderly evacuation of other employees
- Review of emergency action plan. An employer must review the emergency action plan with each employee covered by the plan when the plan is developed or the employee is assigned initially to a job; when the employee's responsibilities under the plan change; and when the plan is changed.

Simpler is better: a short summary of procedures is more useful than a fat binder that never gets read. In addition to the above, you may need to consider

- Special responsibilities: protecting data, securing hazardous operations or equipment
- Special needs employees (consider a buddy system)
- Emergency supplies and materials (establishing and maintaining)
- Data backup. Most businesses rely on computer data. Computing needs may include financial and accounting information, materials planning and ordering, shipping and transportation information,

and client lists. Some high-tech companies also have expensive specialty software. Establish a data backup plan that makes copies of this information on a regular basis (daily, weekly, monthly, or some combination) and store backup data off site. This may require the purchase of a backup storage device and/or software, but many effective options are inexpensive. As part of your data backup plan, consider what paper documents are important and make copies to store off site or in a fireproof safe. Don't forget a complete inventory of equipment and materials;

- Relocation plan. Gather your key personnel for a brainstorming session. If your present place of business were suddenly unavailable, how would you stay in business? One small engineering firm suffered a fire one night, but by the end of the next day, they had rented temporary space, recovered data, and were functioning at a bare bones level. What are your core functions? What are the critical data sources? Where could you move and at what cost? You may never have to implement the plan, but the exercise may identify areas to focus on in your planning.

Prepare to Recover Quickly

- **Insurance:** One key part of your disaster preparedness is insurance. Review existing policies with your agent and learn exactly what coverage you currently have. Determine if you need other kinds of insurance. In addition to property (be sure you have replacement value) and liability, consider loss-of-business insurance. Offices within residences have special insurance considerations. Some homeowner's policies have limitations on coverage that a business might need. Review your needs with your agent.

- **Communications:** After a disaster that affects your business, you will need to figure out how it affects your suppliers and how it may affect your clients. Quick contact to both sides of the equation will take the uncertainty out of the situation and will significantly reduce your—and their—stress. Decide whom you would need to call and keep a paper copy of the list handy. Include banks, debtors, and creditors as well. Remember that electronic databases may by inoperative in those first few hours or days. Many businesses also find it difficult to get the word out after a disaster that they are open for business. Consider how you generate clients; if you depend on street traffic, a sign may be best. If you have business clients, consider a phone campaign to contact and assure them.

- **Response**: After a disaster strikes, keep breathing. Experts warn that the shock of a disaster will affect even the most stoic of people. Take a few deep breaths, gather your team, and begin to assess and plan. When cleaning up after a disaster, avoid physically overdoing it. There may be a million things to do, but they will be more difficult if you have a heart attack. Take pictures, make notes, and keep receipts of everything you do related to recovery. If the government declares a disaster, you may be eligible for assistance of some kind. The records will also help when dealing with insurance adjusters.

• • •

An emergency doesn't have to mean the end of your business—that would be a disaster indeed.

Emergency preparedness: Do one thing today.

COMMUNICATIONS IN AN EMERGENCY

Communities, first responders, and rescue organizations constantly practice emergency response skills. Sometimes they practice around a table. Sometimes they practice with other emergency organizations. Sometimes they practice full-scale, with volunteer victims and fake injuries. In all cases, the main thing they are practicing is communications. Of course, we are talking about organizations that use widely different communications equipment and different frequencies and protocols. But the lesson is still clear for us: effective response to emergencies is all about communications. Here are a few ideas about keeping information flowing in an emergency.

Personal Communications

Every 72-hour kit should have a battery-powered AM/FM radio, with fresh batteries. Better if it is also powered by solar cells or hand crank. The radio will keep you in touch with the most reliable sources of news and leave you less susceptible to rumors. It is useful to also have a list of local radio stations. Check the Internet for a listing by format and dial location, print a copy, and store it with the radio.

Another useful item for your 72-hour kit is a collection of recent family photos. If you need the authorities to help you locate a lost member of your family, a photo with a physical description may hasten the search.

Family Communications

In any emergency, you want to check on your own family and then let them know you are okay. Many disasters, such as earthquakes or power outages, may make it difficult for you to contact each other directly. And if evacuating, you may not even have access to a phone for some time. Identify a friend or relative outside of the immediate area (preferably outside the state) that everyone in the family can call to relay messages. This out-of-state contact person can act as a message board and write down where the caller is, what time they called, where they are going, what route they will use, when they will call again, and so on. Make sure everyone has a copy of key phone numbers and knows when and how to use them. Since cell phones may not work and you may have to rely on now-disappearing public phones, tape phone money to the list that has the phone numbers on it.

Neighborhood Communications

In a larger emergency, neighborhoods will likely band together to help each other. Communicating in this larger area, however, requires different tools. Before an emergency, some neighborhoods have established "phone trees" to help get the word out. In these systems, one person calls two people, who each call two more, and so on until everyone has been alerted. While useful in many situations, phone trees are vulnerable to single-point failures: if someone in the line is not home or neglects to make their calls, some people may not get the message. Be sure to build some flexibility into your phone tree if you choose this method.

During a disaster, the most reliable neighborhood approach is the old "sneakernet": information transmitted by runners. This system works at the neighborhood scale, even when roads may be impassable. To reduce the possibility of miscommunications, make sure all messages are written clearly and legibly. Keep a small pad of paper and a pencil in your 72-hour kit. (If you store a pen, replace it often to keep it from drying out.)

If cell phones are inoperative, as they were for wide areas right after Superstorm Sandy, you can still use local-area radios, known as FRS radios. For a modest investment, you can have a walkie-talkie with a radius of several blocks. Radios by a number of different manufacturers share the same frequency ranges, so coordinating with others in your neighborhood requires that you select a common frequency that everyone can use. Remember that FRS radio transmissions are open to anyone with a radio; they do not provide private or secure conversations. These radios are also useful in neighborhood searches or watches.

Communications with Authorities

Obviously, if the phone system works, calls for assistance can be made on the 911 system. If telephones are not functional, emergency responders, like the fire department, sheriff's office, and police department, all have radio systems. As noted above, they practice frequently to make sure they can coordinate with each other. Less well known is a network of amateur HAM radio operators who are also organized and constantly training to assist in case an emergency disables standard communications. In Hurricane Katrina, sometimes the only functional communications were through HAM radio operators, who even functioned as 911 dispatchers. HAM operators may be attached to city emergency operations centers, various emergency organizations, and other public services, such as shelters. Amateur radio organizations welcome new members, and many clubs even sponsor training to help the new member qualify for a license. Amateur radio organizations frequently participate in large-area disaster drills to improve their effectiveness in a real emergency.

• • •

One last note about communications: information is only as useful as it is accurate. If you have a message that needs to be transmitted, it may be helpful to include your source: "I heard on radio WABC that . . .," or "The mayor just reported that . . .," or "The fire department recommends. . . ." That way, the recipient can evaluate the information and pursue additional confirmation, if warranted.

Emergency preparedness: Do one thing today.

CAMPING: A GREAT PREPAREDNESS HOBBY

No electricity. No running water. No flushing toilet. You carry every-thing and depend on yourself. You find water, but you dare not drink until you purify it. With no place to buy food, you make a one-pot casserole from your meager stores. It's okay—the simpler the meal, the less fuel you use. Night comes on. You'll need shelter against the cold or maybe a storm. You protect your food from animals and judge that you have enough for an evening treat. Cradling a hot drink, you revel in another gorgeous sunset and wonder if you should start a fire tonight.

No, I'm not describing an end-of-the-world scenario. I'm describing a campout. Few family activities are as useful for practicing emergency preparedness skills as camping. Backpacking is even better. Here's why:

Camping Fosters Preparedness Attitudes

When you camp, you develop attitudes and perspectives that are different from a comfortable life at home. For example, you must get used to thinking ahead. Wilderness is usually far from the supermar-ket. You have to think through your trip and get supplies beforehand. Inevitably you will forget something or an unforeseen situation will arise, so you must also develop an attitude of improvising—make do with what you have. And often you discover that not as many things are necessary to your life as you thought, which is another good prepared-ness attitude. In fact, camping helps distinguish between basics and luxuries. Other beneficial attitudes you develop while camping include self-reliance, discipline, and the concept that you can do without con-stant comfort or immediate gratification.

Camping Develops Preparedness Skills

People who camp develop skills that are useful in emergencies. Backpacking is especially good because of the total separation from civilization. Campers learn to estimate types of supplies and necessary quantities. You learn to minimize excess and waste. One key skill is to see which compromises will save weight or complexity. Extreme example: backpackers who save pounds of stoves and gear by planning only no-cook meals. Frequent campers also learn how to conserve fuel, minimize messes, use less water, and ration personal energy to get everything done.

Other skills include cooking with dried foods, one-pan cooking, spicing up bland or repetitive meals, water purification, and pest avoidance. Skills like choosing a campsite, seeking shelter, and organizing a camp could be handy if you were displaced from home. Building a fire with a variety of fuels and tools—and only one match—is harder than it looks. And learning methods of reducing your exposure to severe weather could literally be lifesaving.

Camping Gets You Equipped

Accumulating great equipment is a key preparedness benefit of camping. All camping gear is emergency gear. The equipment gets the most benefit out of the smallest volume or weight. Be careful, you can spend a lot on equipment that is not right for your family or camping style. Define your needs before shopping. Are you going to camp from a car? Then weight and bulk are not as important. Are you going to camp at undeveloped sites? Then you'll need to take water and sanitation into account. Are you going to camp yearly or weekly? Shop around and be patient. Discontinued styles or last year's models have extra discounts, and if they were good enough last year, they'll be fine this year. With research (outdoors magazines usually have primers on buying gear) you can identify the features you need and pick up some great gear. Here are some additional tips:

- **Tents:** You don't need to buy a blizzard-resistant model (expensive), but the rain fly should cover the tent and be waterproof, not just water resistant. Best buy: a three-season tent. Climb in before you buy—not all two-man tents fit two men. Other handy features are a freestanding design and a large vestibule. Make sure it's easy to set up in the dark and that it is sturdy; breaking a tent pole on a rainy night is not fun.

- **Sleeping bags**: Rectangular bags are roomier. Mummy bags are usually warmer. Get one that fits—if it is too big, you will be cold; if it is too small, you'll be uncomfortable. Temperature ratings are only a guideline, not a guarantee. Down fill is warmer (and more expensive), but synthetic fibers insulate even when wet. Don't forget a sleeping pad; it will not only ease the hardness of the ground, it will also insulate for more warmth. Closed-cell foam pads are cheap and light; self-inflating pads are comfy and don't take much space.

- **Clothes**: Clothes should be worn in layers. In cold weather, wear synthetic materials next to your skin; cotton stays wet, and you get chilled. Synthetic fleece is good for a middle insulating layer since it is light and insulates even when wet, like wool. The outer layer should be waterproof, not just water resistant. Don't forget a knit cap, and remember that cheap mittens (fleece works well) are warmer than expensive gloves.

- **Cooking gear, stove**: Spending a lot on stoves is easy, and most veteran campers try several types before finding a favorite, so ask your friends. The varieties are mostly based on type of fuel and adjustability of the flame. A versatile cooking kit contains a couple of pots, a lid/frying pan, and a handle. Add some insulated plastic mugs, spoons, and a pocketknife.

- **Water purification**: No stream or lake is guaranteed to be drinkable. Purify by heat (bring to a rolling boil), chlorine (eight drops unscented Clorox per gallon), iodine tablets, or filters. If you pick a filter, don't skimp; get one guaranteed to remove giardia. A carbon add-on filter will help the water taste better too.

Camping for Better Emergency Preparedness

If you have camped before, try it again. If you haven't, start slow. First, go to a developed campsite with toilets and water. After you are comfortable creating your own light, heat, and shelter, try a "dry camp" where you take your own water and sanitary arrangements. If you want even more challenge, camp in the wilderness. Safety advice: don't try summer desert camping or winter mountain camping without instruction and proper equipment.

• • •

Be sure to practice low-impact camping: camp two hundred feet away from water; use established campsites and fire rings; bring your own firewood; don't trench around tents; don't cut live trees; try to stay off vegetation; and leave each campsite and trail cleaner than you found it.

Chances are that your first camping trip will have surprises, so go with an attitude of adventure. You probably know some accomplished campers; learn from the experts. But the best advice for learning preparedness skills is to camp, camp, camp.

Emergency preparedness:
Do one thing today.

ADAPTABILITY: LESSONS OF A BANDANNA

103 Uses for a Bandanna

In virtually all lists of emergency kits of all kinds in this book, a bandanna is listed as a key item. The reason for this is simple: the bandanna is cheap, versatile, and adaptable. In everyday life as well as emergency situations, the common cotton bandanna is unrivaled in the number and type of functions: medical, personal hygiene, survival, food preparation, clothing, repair, and so on. One hundred and three uses are listed here, but the list could surely go on and on. The bandanna demonstrates a key survival principle: resourcefulness. You may not have all of the things you want on hand, but if you can adapt a little and be creative with what you do have—like bandannas—you can probably make a go of it.

When buying bandannas, look for 100 percent cotton, get a color that isn't embarrassing to you, and look for the larger sizes. Buy several and place them in your cars, 72-hour kits, coat pockets, desk drawers at work, first-aid kits, camping gear, fanny packs, school backpacks, lockers, boats, campers, trailers, and so on.

First Aid

1. **Bandage:** use as a compress on a bleeding wound.

2. **Tie:** hold a pressure bandage in place.

3. **Sling:** tie opposite corners together, sling over neck, and insert arm. Use two more bandannas tied end-to-end to immobilize sling against chest.

4. **Finger splint:** tape or tie folded bandanna around injured finger to immobilize.

5. **Splint tie:** rip into strips to secure splints against limbs.

6. **Poultice:** fill with clean, cool mud or damp sand for bug bite or minor burn relief.

7. **Tourniquet tie:** use only if life is in immediate danger.

8. **Snake bite band:** tie two to four inches above bite to slow the spread of venom.

9. **Ankle wrap:** tie a snug crossing pattern around the ankle and over the shoe to give support to twisted ankle.

10. **Wrist brace:** wrap around wrist joint for extra support.

11. **Sponge:** use to clean around wounds.

12. **Face cloth:** dampen and use to relieve fever or swelling.

13. **Hot pack:** dip in warm water and apply to skin.

14. **Cold pack:** fill with ice and apply to injury.

Clothing

15. **Hat:** make a sun cover for head, pirate style. Soak with water to cool.

16. **Ear muffs:** tie as a wide headband and pull down over ears.

17. **Mittens:** wrap around fingers to protect from wind chill.

18. **Work gloves:** wrap around the hands to minimize blisters.

19. **Winter scarf:** tie loosely around neck to slow heat flow out of parka.

20. **Summer scarf:** tie around neck to prevent sunburn.

21. **Belt:** tie end-to-end. Some waists may need two or three bandannas.

22. **Sweatband:** tie around forehead or wrists.

23. **Dust mask:** make a "train robber" mask. Also works in winter to warm face.

24. **Sock:** wrap around foot and insert into shoe.

25. **Shoelaces**: rip into strips and roll up.

26. **Patches**: subdivide to patch several holes in clothing.

27. **Boot padding**: stuff in toe of oversize shoe or boot.

28. **Strap padding**: use folded bandannas to provide extra padding under backpack straps and such.

29. **Knee pad**: tie or tape folded bandannas to knees for canoeing and such.

30. **Insulation**: fold up and lay on bottom of each boot for extra warmth.

31. **Sunglasses**: poke small holes and tie across face to reduce the glare of sun on snow.

32. **Glasses strap**: tie one end to each earpiece.

33. **Purse**: wrap personal valuables.

34. **Watchband**: rip a strip and tie around band pins to replace a broken band.

35. **Hair tie**: you'll feel better when you look better.

Food Preparation and Cleanup

36. **Dishcloth**: fold several times to use as a scrubber. Add some sand to increase effectiveness.

37. **Dish towel**: dry dishes directly, or lay out flat to lay clean utensils on.

38. **Apron**: tuck in the front of waistband.

39. **Hot pad**: fold several times to insulate fingers from hot pans.

40. **Tablecloth**: lay bandanna out flat to prepare food on.

41. **Seat cover**: lay bandanna out flat to sit on.

42. **Steamer**: stretch over top of pan with small amount of water and place vegetables on cloth and lid on top of that.

43. **Strainer**: use to drain water from vegetables, pasta, and so on.

44. **Food wrap**: wrap up bread or other food temporarily.

45. **Bug cover**: lay over dishes of food to keep insects off until serving time.

46. **Bib:** tie loosely around neck.

47. **Napkin/wipe:** for messes on hands and faces.

48. **Tea bag:** use to mull spices or teas.

49. **Trash container:** wrap up scraps and garbage until you get to a real can.

50. **Water strainer:** will not purify water, but will remove large contaminants.

51. **Sterilizer:** wrap baby bottle nipples and such in bandanna and dip into boiling water.

52. **Wick clarifier:** clarifies (does not purify) murky or silty water by wicking from a high container to a lower one.

Personal Hygiene

53. **Washcloth:** if used for personal hygiene, don't use for food preparation.

54. **Towel:** to dry off. May need to wring it out several times.

55. **Handkerchief:** like it was designed!

56. **Diaper:** dispose after use.

57. **Toilet paper:** rip into small pieces. Dispose after use.

58. **Feminine hygiene:** if out of supplies.

59. **Toothbrush:** dab a corner in water and scrub teeth.

Survival

60. **Shade:** protect tender skin from sunburn.

61. **Fire windscreen:** rig to protect a match or infant fire.

62. **Fire starter:** shred to provide dry tinder.

63. **Fire wick:** twist a small piece into string and use with wax to make a candle.

64. **Cord/rope:** rip into strips and tie end to end.

65. **Lashing:** rip into strips to lash sticks into tools and utensils.

66. **Small-game snare:** lay it over a small pit trap and cover with leaves, or make a fling snare.

67. **Sling**: make a primitive slingshot, David-and-Goliath-style.

68. **Pack**: wrap up items and tie to a stick, hobo-style.

69. **Stuff sack**: keep small personal items together in pack or container.

70. **Signal**: display against contrasting background.

71. **Flashlight cover**: put different colors over flashlight to send colored signals.

72. **Trail marker**: put small bits on the tops of rock cairns to show the way you went.

73. **Notepaper**: light colors work to leave notes if you use ink.

74. **Tie**: repair tents, packs, clothes, gear, and so on.

75. **Tie down**: lash gear to pack or canoe.

76. **Bear bag**: suspend food in one or more bandannas to keep animals out.

77. **Throwing weight**: fill with dirt or rocks, tie to one end of bear bag rope, and throw over a sturdy branch to anchor the bag.

Miscellaneous

78. **Pillow**: lay a clean cover over other stuff.

79. **Earplugs**: for sleeping in noisy public shelters.

80. **Kite tail**: you never know when this will be a sanity saver.

81. **Blindfold**: use to sleep in a lighted shelter or play games.

82. **Parachute toy**: tie corners to a small weight, roll up, and toss.

83. **Windsock**: tie corners together to make a drag chute.

84. **Magic tricks**: use to distract bored children.

85. **Puppet**: use rubber bands to create features.

86. **Doll clothes**: you never know when you'll need this distraction.

87. **Game pieces**: tear some pieces to play checkers, for example.

88. **Ball or Hacky Sack**: fill with stuffing and tie tightly.

89. **Car antenna marker**: tie to radio antenna in a large parking lot.

90. **Bookmark**: use a single thread.

91. **Glasses cleaner:** sometimes you just need a clean, soft cloth.

92. **Specimen holder:** wrap up shells, leaves, pinecones, rocks, or whatever is being collected.

93. **Baby pacifier:** soak a corner in water or juice and let baby suck on it.

94. **Applicator:** use to apply paint, stain, grease, and so on.

95. **Broom:** use to sweep up a small floor area.

96. **Dustpan:** hold down the front edge and sweep dirt up onto the bandanna.

97. **Mop:** dampen, fold, and wipe a floor area.

98. **Burp cloth:** what parent hasn't needed an extra one of these?

99. **Window wipe:** clean grime, smudges, or fog off the inside of car windows.

100. **Car window shade:** close the window on one side of the bandanna. Be sure not to obscure driver's view.

101. **Plumb bob:** fill with sand or dirt, tie ends together, and suspend from string.

102. **Pet collar:** be careful not to tie too tightly.

103. **Gift wrap:** give a bandanna to someone you know as the wrapping for another gift.

• • •

The bandanna is a versatile tool, the uses of which are limited only by your resourcefulness.

Emergency preparedness: Buy one bandanna today.

EMERGENCY PREPAREDNESS GIFT IDEAS

Gift holidays, like Christmas, are a great time to augment your emergency preparedness. Here are some gift ideas for just about everyone:

Dutch Ovens

Everyone loves a Dutch oven meal, in any season. Dutch ovens also increase your cooking options in an emergency. With a little charcoal or a wood fire, you can cook a variety of outdoor meals easily (never use charcoal indoors). Some Dutch oven supplies that make great gifts include

- Dutch oven: Don't scrimp here. Buy a good cast-iron oven with uniform wall thickness, well-fitting lid with a lip on the top, sturdy legs, and handle. The size you choose depends upon the size of crowd you want to cook for. Four to six hungry people can eat from a twelve- to fourteen-inch oven.

- Tools: Dutch oven cooking is made easier with the right tools, including a charcoal starter; a small shovel; coal tongs; heavy leather gloves; lid lifter; lid rest; and outdoor cooking box with spatulas, spoons, oven mitts, spices, paper towels, and so on.

- Cookbooks: Even the most experienced Dutch oven cook is always looking for new recipes. Choose from the basic to the exotic among the many Dutch oven cookbooks on the market. See "Additional Resources" at the end of the book for some Dutch oven cookbook recommendations.

- Other: A Dutch oven hearth and windbreak are also useful. Buy a commercial charcoal holder/windbreak, or make your own.

Camping Gear

Any camping gear adds to your family preparedness. A lot of camping gear is also lightweight for backpackers, which makes it more versatile in your preparedness inventory.

- Backpacks/day packs (carry emergency gear)
- Tents (emergency shelter)
- Sleeping bags/pads/camp pillows (a good night's sleep in an emergency is invaluable)
- Water filters (make an emergency water source drinkable)
- Stoves/cooking kits (emergency cooking)
- Warm, versatile clothing (emergencies don't always happen on sunny spring days)
- Flashlights and battery lanterns (emergency lighting)

Emergency Kits

You can assemble a variety of kits for emergency preparedness. An advantage to this type of gift is you can buy individual items as you find them on sale, and you can tailor the gift to your budget.

- 72-hour kit: See chapter 3
- Car kit: Tools and emergency supplies that you might need if you broke down or were stranded
- Office kit: A mini 72-hour kit for that extra drawer in your office.
- First-aid kit: This can range from a small pocket kit for hikes to a fully equipped home or car kit to cover a wide range of emergencies

Service Gift Certificates

Homemade gift certificates are always a fun idea and can be inexpensive. Try certificates for

- Quarterly smoke detector checks; function and battery
- Water supply rotation
- Water heater tie-down

- Lights-out practice and candle-lit dinner
- Emergency preparedness files organizing

Stocking Stuffers

For a limited budget, you can also get some emergency preparedness stocking stuffers for Christmas:

- Space blanket/bag for car or pocket kit
- Signaling whistle
- Pocket heat packs
- Emergency radio; powered by battery, hand crank, or solar
- Light sticks
- Inexpensive flashlight
- Pocketknife
- Emergency gloves, hat, or socks

Other

Other gift ideas include:

- Good LED lantern; battery powered
- High-quality, heavy-duty, no-kidding emergency flashlight (and batteries)
- Anything for the food preserver in your family: pressure canner; juicer; applesauce maker; food dryer; vacuum sealer; jar lifter.
- Multipurpose pliers/tools. Be sure to get a good quality tool; many cheap brands don't fit together well and won't last long.
- Emergency preparedness books. Any bookstore or emergency preparedness specialty store will carry a good selection.

• • •

A little imagination can result in useful and much appreciated gifts. The possibilities are endless.

Emergency preparedness:
Do one thing today.

CONCLUSION

No-Cost Emergency Preparedness Tips

Too many people think of emergency preparedness as overwhelming, complex, difficult, and time-consuming. We think we are so busy that we don't have time; we think we are living so close to the edge that we don't have the money. But there are a huge number of things you can do—today!—that are free, simple, and helpful. Some of them don't even take much time. Here are fifteen:

1. Wear your seat belt—everybody, every trip. This may not prevent an earthquake, but it could reduce a car accident to a mere inconvenience.

2. Stop smoking, eat right, exercise, and get enough sleep. Don't underestimate the effect your health can have on you and your family. A healthy person is able to weather the stresses of other kinds of crises.

3. Do a hazards hunt in your home. Take a pencil and paper and walk through your house noting conditions that may be unsafe. Check for fire hazards; hazardous materials; unsafe or unstable furniture; and access to medicines, chemicals, dangerous tools, or paints and solvents. Most household hazards can be corrected with some simple cleaning or rearranging.

4. Create a fire evacuation plan. Pick two ways to get out of every room. Make sure you have tools for safely opening (or breaking) windows, and ladders if required. Designate a location to gather outside of the house. Teach everyone how to call 911, and when.

Teach kids how to test for fire beyond a door; how to crawl to a window; and how to stop, drop, and roll. Practice your evacuation.

5. Teach utility shutoff skills. Teach everyone old enough where to turn off the electricity, water, and gas. Teach them *when* to turn it off and when not. Practice, but don't really turn off the gas since a plumber or gas company employee will have to come and turn it back on and light the pilot lights.

6. Practice flame safety. Never leave candles burning unattended. Don't let children play with matches or candles. Put away matches and lighters. Consciously teach fire safety to kids.

7. Create a family plan. Write down your out-of-state contact, the person everyone will call in an emergency. Write down other emergency numbers and make a copy for each member of the family. Figure out how and where you'll all get together after an emergency. Don't forget to designate a second place outside of your neighborhood in case your house is inaccessible. Plan out what other things you would like to do to get ready, including 72-hour kits, food and water storage, and emergency and first-aid training.

8. Learn your children's school emergency response plan. Learn your workplace emergency response plan.

9. Network with your neighbors. A neighborhood is an awesome resource, but you must work out how you can cooperate with and watch out for each other. Getting to know your neighbors is the first thing to do. Agreeing to something as simple as checking each other's utilities or pets in an emergency is a real step forward.

10. Sleep with a flashlight and pair of shoes next to your bed. Even a mild earthquake can knock out the power and create serious hazards for bare feet.

11. Learn something new about some aspect of emergency preparedness you are especially worried about or interested in. Libraries have books on the shelves and other books available by requesting transfers from other libraries. The Internet has many sites, some better than others, chock-full of good information. Try the American Red Cross site or ready.gov, or search for "emergency preparedness."

12. Practice. Eat a meal out of your 72-hour kit. How does it taste? Have a lights-out practice. Do you really know where that flashlight is?

Does it work? How will you entertain yourself and the kids without electricity?

13. Organize and protect your important papers: deeds, titles, insurance policies, contracts, mortgages, and so on.

14. Learn to make your own non-technological fun. Learn to play simple games with few pieces or parts. Collect instructions for card games and parlor games. Store dice, playing cards, pencil and paper, and other items that support a variety of different games.

15. When staying in a hotel, read the evacuation plan fixed to the door. In restaurants and bars, note where the closest doors are. When you go to public places or events, get into the habit of mentally choosing a primary and backup exit in case of emergency.

These are just a few of the many things you can do to get ready for an emergency that don't take a lot of time and don't cost a lot of money. After you do one of them, choose another one to do tomorrow; emergency preparedness is an ongoing process.

Four Principles to Keep You Going

Understanding four key principles of emergency preparedness can keep us going when obstacles like apathy, confusion, and discouragement get in our way. Keeping these principles in mind will help you avoid distorting emergency preparedness, getting distracted from your objectives, or even overdoing it.

Principle #1

The objective of preparation is to keep bad situations from becoming worse. Preparing is about giving yourself options in a bad situation. This changes your attitude from victim to survivor. The knowledge that you have not used the last of the tricks in your bag can stave off panic. Almost no situation gets better if you panic; hysteria is not our friend. Two examples:

- A retired couple exploring back roads of southern Utah late one autumn encountered some difficulty on a dirt road. They stayed with the car for several days but finally decided to walk for it. The strain was too much for the man, and he died of a heart attack before help arrived. A bad situation got worse.

- One January, a mother dropped her car off for maintenance and walked several blocks to the school to pick up a child. The sun was shining, the air calm. It felt like spring. She met the child and started back just as a stiff breeze kicked up and the sun disappeared. In an instant, spring returned to winter. They were not dressed for it. The child got cold and refused to walk. They were blocks away from the car, and it was very cold. A now-frightened mother picked up the child and ran, walked, and finally limped back to the car. This story ended happily. But a bad situation could have become worse.

Many bad situations could get worse, ranging from personal emergencies like house fires and becoming lost or stranded to neighborhood or wide-area emergencies like floods, storms, chemical spills, or earthquakes. Sometimes it seems like the world is a minefield and we're doing the polka in snowshoes, but if you remind yourself that these are bad situations that you may not be able to prevent, all you really have to do is ask yourself what you could do now to prevent them from going from bad to worse.

Principle #2

Any preparation is better than no preparation. It doesn't have to be perfect. Here's why: you can't possibly know everything to prepare for, and there is no way to know what perfect is. Further, each family will not be alone, even in the worst scenario. We live in neighborhoods and communities. We will still be able to trade, barter, and help each other. So, armed with the knowledge that all you are trying to do is keep bad things from getting worse and now realizing that it doesn't have to be perfect, you're probably already better off than you think. Anything you do is right. Anything you prepare, including knowledge, pushes you forward. Here are some things to keep in mind:

- Tailor your preparedness to your own family—have a meeting or informal discussion. You probably already know what you need to work on next. If you are just starting out, try discussing fire safety and develop an escape plan. Learn where utility shutoffs are located. If you are more advanced, test yourselves and your preparation with a practice.

- Prepare to have some comfort and some fun too. It actually doesn't take too much to survive. It takes a bit more to survive without whining. Most of our preparation turns out to be creating comfort and convenience. Think about what it would take to have your family regard an emergency less like an ordeal and more like an adventure. It is good advice to store a game or two and to store fewer sawdust cookies and more pudding cups.

- Since you can't prepare for everything, you've got to be flexible; go for multiple solutions. You can prepare several kinds of light sources, for example, or several ways to cook your food.

Principle #3

Do one thing today. As trite as it sounds, and as tired of it as you may be by now, this is the most potent emergency preparedness advice in this book. It counters distraction by letting you focus on one thing, no matter what it is, and by doing it every day. Preparedness means not procrastinating. And key to not procrastinating is getting started, no matter how small the step. Involve everyone and return to it often.

Principle #4

Less can sometimes be more. Don't overdo it. Especially don't overplan it. Having an imperfect grab-and-go box is better than having a plan for a perfect, color-coordinated 72-hour kit. Having one flashlight that works is better than having a dozen in various states of disrepair. You get the idea.

• • •

Besides getting prepared, there are other rewards. Emergency preparedness gives us perspective: we acknowledge that nothing is permanent and things can change. And things change not only for the worse but also the better—when things are bad, we know that "this too shall pass." If we involve our families, preparedness can teach our children to put something away for a rainy day. This is a worthwhile lesson considering that advertisers constantly howl at them to seek immediate gratification. Finally, emergency preparedness gives us confidence that can spill over into other parts of our lives.

Emergency preparedness: Do one thing today.

ADDITIONAL RESOURCES

This book is not meant to be comprehensive. For those interested, a number of additional resources are available from which advanced information can be obtained. Public organizations as well as published literature are all available. Also, I regularly highlight interesting and topical information, and include updates and reviews on the Do One Thing Today site at familypreparation.blogspot.com.

In all cases, remember: *caveat emptor*, "let the buyer beware." This is because information sources can be outdated or inaccurate. With preparedness information, you must constantly update and expand.

Websites

- http://familypreparation.blogspot.com
- http://www.redcross.org
- http://www.ready.gov (FEMA)
- http://www.bt.cdc.gov (Centers for Disease Control and Prevention)
- http://publicsafety.utah.gov/emergencymanagement
- http://www.usgs.gov (US Geological Survey)
- http://www.nrc.gov/about-nrc/emerg-preparedness.html (US Nuclear Regulatory Commission)
- http://www.fsis.usda.gov/FACTSheets/Emergency_Preparedness_Fact_Sheets/index.asp (Food Safety and Inspection Service)

Books

- *Are You Ready? An In-Depth Guide to Citizen Preparedness*, Federal Emergency Management Agency, 2013.

- Bouwman, Fred, *The Practical Camp Cook*, Cedar Fort Publishing, 2005.

- *Boy Scout Handbook*, 12th ed., Boy Scouts of America, 2009.

- Briscoe, Alan K., *Your Guide to Emergency Home Storage*, Cedar Fort Publishing, 2009.

- Dickey, Esther, *Skills for Survival: How Families Can Prepare*, Cedar Fort Publishing, 2009.

- *Fieldbook: The BSA's Manual of Advanced Skills for Outdoor Travel, Adventure, and Caring for the Land*, 4th ed., Boy Scouts of America, 2004.

- Jaynes, Blair D., *Emergency Survival Packs: How to Prepare a Fourteen-Day Evacuation Kit*, Horizon Publishers, 1982.

- Lee, Brent, *Living for Tomorrow*, Cedar Fort Publishing, 2009.

- *Putting Down Roots in Earthquake Country: Your Handbook for Earthquakes in Utah*, Utah Seismic Safety Commission, 2008.

- Rawlings, Marla, *The Beginner's Guide to Dutch Oven Cooking*, Cedar Fort Publishing, 2012.

- Read, Teena, *Family Emergency Preparedness Plan*, Cedar Fort Publishing, 2008.

- Ririe, Robert L., *Doin' Dutch Oven*, Cedar Fort Publishing, 2012.

- Salsbury, Barbara, *It's Time to Plan, Not Panic*, Cedar Fort Publishing, 2006.

- Salsbury, Barbara, *Preparedness Principles: The Complete Personal Preparedness Resource Guide for Any Emergency Situation*, Cedar Fort Publishing, 2006.

- Schimelpfenig, Todd, *NOLS Wilderness Medicine*, 5th ed., Stackpole Books, 2013.

- South, J. Allan, *The Sense of Survival*, Timpanogos Publishers, 1986.

Other

- County extension service: Information about growing and preserving food.
- Electrical utility: Information about electrical safety.
- Fire department: Fire safety and prevention, hazmat response.
- Gas utility: Gas safety, water heater tips, shutoff info.
- Insurance agent: Insurance coverage and needs.
- Local government: Community preparedness plans, LEPC.
- Public safety (police/sheriff): Street safety, neighborhood watch.
- State health department: Water purification, epidemics.
- Water utility: Water quality, shutoff info.

• • •

There are additional resources for any topic of interest. Search in your local library, in your favorite bookstore, or on the Internet using keywords like "emergency," "disaster," "survival," "food storage," "prepare." Or do a search on your area of specific interest: hurricanes, earthquakes, tornadoes, and so on. Emergency preparedness is all about information.

Emergency preparedness:
Do one thing today.

INDEX

ABOUT THE AUTHOR

EVAN GABRIELSEN started writing articles about emergency preparedness to counter circulating misperceptions and misinformation, even before the Internet. His monthly columns on which much of this book is based were first published in the *Valley Journals* on Utah's Wasatch Front. He has presented preparedness concepts to numerous groups and organizations.

The years of research convinced him that there was a need for a balanced, accurate, and common-sense resource for families just starting out, and this book was born. He wanted to compile basic information for families seeking self-reliance without being extremists. The result is a book that is easy to read, motivating, and able to help any family get just a little better prepared for the disasters that will surely come to all.

Gabe received a bachelor's degree in mechanical engineering from Brigham Young University in 1983, and he has worked on booster rockets, demilitarization, advanced materials, and environmental cleanup projects. He is a licensed engineer and has written numerous papers and presentations for technical and professional organizations.

He and his wife are the parents of two children and three grandchildren. He enjoys reading, writing, camping, and traveling, especially to see the grandchildren. Oh, and just like in the first edition, he still spends time leading Boy Scouts.

Do one thing today at familypreparation.blogspot.com.